Do *NOT* Invent Buggy Whips

Kenneth J. Thurber

Do NOT Invent Buggy Whips

Create!
Reinvent!
Position!
Disrupt!

Kenneth J. Thurber Ph.D.

ISBN 13: 978-0-9833424-3-4

Library of Congress Control Number: 2012930814

Cover Illustration by Shawn McCann
Book design and typesetting by James Monroe Design, LLC.

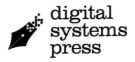

Digital Systems Press
33 Thornwood Drive, Suite 500
Ithaca, NY 14850
www.digitalsystemspress.com

Do Not Invent Buggy Whips:
www.DoNotInventBuggyWhips.com

To my wife.

Contents

Preface

After writing *Big Wave Surfing: Extreme Technology Development, Management, Marketing and Investing* (BWS), I thought that I had answered most of the questions that my friends had asked me over the years. I soon found out that the book raised more questions than it answered. Most of the questions dealt with whether an individual could cause or create a big wave. My answer, and view, is YES! With imagination, creativity and discipline, it is possible to create a new big wave and the technology arena is the place to go to make that happen. The other major question was how do people innovate and how do you define innovation.

As I spoke at conferences and provided interviews, the themes that constantly developed were how do you create a big wave? How do you spot a big wave? How do you avoid a wipeout? I never thought of these issues as complex because from my position these were just things that happened and you either participated or spotted the trend and latched onto it or you missed the wave and quite possibly a chance to make a good living.

When BWS debuted, the stock market was highly volatile and there was growing social unrest. In December 2010, we predicted the unrest on Wall Street when the book went to the printer. Even then we did not understand the potential size of the occupy movement, although we perceived it as more violent than it has been to date (December 2011). Big waves were coming in a lot of areas.

Due to pressures of the market place one of the companies that I was leading was going into a market that required a lot of foresight and the best way for them to survive was to be very innovative. I found myself trying to make people think way "outside the box" and take serious risks to ensure that we were perceived as leading thinkers, developers and product sellers in various advanced computer network market spaces.

As I tried to encourage my employees, it became a process of trying to develop in them the ability to articulate and focus their thinking on the issues of innovation. What constitutes the ability to set in place a trend or create a product that is truly unique became a serious topic of interest. In particular, what is product innovation and how would you decide that a product was innovative. This became the focus of a series of discussions that spanned a number of years—both prior to and after the Big Wave Surfing Book's publication.

My claim is that if you are serious about creating a big wave you must focus on the concept of market disruption!

Over the years I have been exposed to a large number of strategies and the people who try to implement them. Eventually, either for survival or to make my life easier, I developed a framework that is useful for thinking about and conceiving a product. That framework is developed and explained in this book. You can use the framework in several ways. You should think of the book as a business tool: a tool that allows you to evaluate business, products and business plans. The book can be used as a "how to" book in the sense it provides a road map which if followed will allow you to develop and evaluate product concepts. The book can also be inspiring and motivational. If you follow its structured system you can overcome your inertia and actually make progress in setting up a product or business concept. The framework in this book allows you to easily examine concepts and conceive of a product.

At its core this book is about disruption. How can you start and develop a disruption? How do you measure the disruption? Can you sell a disruptive technology?

These topics will be modeled and discussed in a framework that I have used to encourage entrepreneurial activities.

This book presents a way of looking at products and not only how to conceive a product but also how to position it. This book is a "how to" guide and if you follow the steps in this book you can work your way through a product strategy and product concept development. It may not be easy but it is possible to do this kind of work if you are motivated. In no way am I suggesting that this is the only way to approach the problem. But, it is one way that I know works and has worked over many years. You will and should develop your own variations of the strategy presented in this book.

Further, inspiration in a majority of cases is really the results of people working hard and being motivated. Some people believe that doing concept work is difficult. My experience is that it is really a matter of going through the process with a serious intent to succeed and staying focused. In many cases people have told me they cannot do the work because they do not know how. If you are not motivated due to a lack of a process, that excuse is no longer valid as I am giving you one way to approach the problem. I know this works! Forty plus years of experience tells me that it works. You have no excuses not to try to better your situation. Further, if you need inspiration, you should realize that not only has this technique worked for me, but it has worked for others that I have taught the strategy. You can improve your status and your situation using the strategy and model described herein!

Do not invent buggy whips. Do not invent film. At some point these were viable products. Where are they today? Where will you be tomorrow?

Buggy whips were integral to the transportation industry of the late 1800s. If you manufactured buggy whips you needed to reinvent yourself and your products. The transportation industry grew, but buggy whips were not the critical element. Some manufacturers survived because they reinvented themselves. Some had moderate success and some went under. The end result was that you needed to be in an evolutionary mode to ensure your success.

The same can be said for film manufacturers. Kodak was a great company and it actually invented digital imaging cameras. Where is it today?

What will happen to hard disk manufacturers?

Where is technology going?

What is the next buggy whip?

There has been innovation in the film and buggy whip businesses. It just ceased and the participants had to find other businesses.

The goal of this book is to show you a way to avoid being a buggy whip manufacturer!

Hopefully, you will embrace the ideas and become very successful.

This book will have no introduction. It will have no conclusion. I do not know where the end is as the discussion always continues.

This book is organized into five parts: origin of ideas and discussion of innovation, model for disruption, application of concepts, examples and, lastly, disruptive future. Each part will consist of a set of chapters that examine the principles discussed in the section. I trust this organization will make the book easy to read.

Acknowledgements

It is not easy to document ideas. What is obvious to one person may look like magic to another. I acknowledge the able assistance of a number of people without whom this book would not be possible: Steve Brueckner, Rob Joyce, Jordan Bonney and Judson Powers (entertaining and informative discussions), Gene Proctor, Julie Baker, Noel Schmidt, Ranga Ramanujan and John Metil (sounding boards and content reviewers) and Paul O'Neill for his contributions to not only the content and ideas but also his extensive contributions to the structure and editing.

PART I

ORIGIN OF IDEAS AND INNOVATION

In this part, we examine several ideas involving the problem of innovation.

We start by discussing innovation and end by discussing how to measure it.

The key point here is that innovation is difficult to measure, identify, quantify and develop until after it has been accepted in the marketplace. Whether something is innovative is a constant debate. Once the public deems it innovative, the argument is over and everybody jumps on the bandwagon. Further, just because something is unique does not make it innovative. It is possible to make products that are so unique that the potential customers do not recognize the need for the product or are not able to conceptualize why the product is useful.

CHAPTER 1

Origin of Ideas

I have often pondered if it's possible to teach someone how to develop a product or whether the understanding necessary to develop a product is native to the person. What do you need to do to develop a product? Can you elaborate on how a product gets developed? These are fundamental questions that may not be answerable. For example, is the process the same for developing a coffee house concept as it is for a new cell phone product?

Many times I have discussed new products with friends who are in the product development business and asked them whether they could explain to me how the product came about. What were the motivating factors? How did they decide which features were needed for a successful product? Where did they get their ideas?

Universally, the product developers could only answer a subset of the questions that I asked. Somehow they developed the product without a lot of thought about the overall process of development. Yet they were able to develop successful products.

Product development is all about trying to bring out a product that will satisfy some real or perceived need. I was complaining to an acquaintance, who was a shrink, about the problem of perception versus reality. The shrink's answer was that if a person perceived reality in a certain way that perception was their reality. In product development if we perceive a need for a product, can we make other people perceive the same need?

Can we create a product reality?

However we decide to answer these questions, the larger question is how we create a disruptive high growth product.

In my opinion, the question of product development only becomes interesting when we try to create products that have a potential to exhibit rapid growth. Rapid growth properly managed provides the way to wealth. In this book we will examine ways of thinking about products and services, but that will evolve into a strategy that focuses on trying to position products so that we can achieve high growth products and see if we can capture market share and sales. In this strategy we will be searching for disruptive technologies. We will try to use them to create products with a rapid growth curve. This is the process that we call creative disruption. We are trying to develop products that make money.

A problem that I have struggled with all of my working life is how to define innovation. I have had the privilege of knowing many people who are considered innovative and who have developed innovative products. Yet there remains this constant question as to what innovation is and how do you measure it. There are lots of books and references to innovation and strategies where people measure and define innovation. Yet these references all recognize innovation after the fact or only discuss theories of innovation.

During my career I have, either as a consultant or designer, been called upon to help people design a new product, develop a new concept or try to explain how to position a new product. Not all of these efforts have yielded innovative products. In some cases innovation consists of features that are perceived as important or desirable relative to the competition. It is with this perception that we can take even a mundane product and position it to be a best-selling product generating wealth.

This is a difficult task as people's definition of innovation differs substantially. In fact there are people who can never see that anything is innovative. At some point, you must define and be able to spot an innovation. If you can do that the next question is whether you can create an innovation technology or an actual innovative product.

No matter what you do some people will not view your idea, product or service as innovative! This happens all the time.

A group that I worked with over the years caused me to think of a huge contradiction in terms of innovation. The company's chief scientist was a brilliant person with a serious problem. He was able to always tell you why something was not innovative. Eventually he could define what he saw as an innovative product. But, his definition relied on him solving all of the technology problems associated with the innovative product. In solving problems he relied upon being able to determine a solution to every possible development obstacle. In fact, he wanted to understand the solution not only in the absolute sense but in the sense of what had already been done in the industry. Think about this. If products are not innovative because they can be described in terms of what had been done before, then how can his innovative idea be innovative if he describes the solution to every problem by how the obstacle was overcome in some other product?

His definition of why a product was not innovative was the problem. His products were never innovative because they were described in terms of products that existed. Yet he could not go forward with a development without knowing that he had an innovative answer. He provided a classic example of the concept of analysis paralysis!

To solve that problem we'll create a range of techniques that can be considered as innovation. And, we will develop a model that will allow us to measure how a product may do if it were to be developed and introduced. In developing that model we will discover how to create disruptive products. Disruption is important because disruptive products can capture sales growth, but they may also not be defensible in terms of a long term growth plan for a company. If your disruption is to simply cut prices then you will face the fate of the airline industry—periodic bankruptcy.

In attempting to define innovation, one needs a framework or model to discuss the process and figure out how to relate disparate ideas. This is a really difficult problem as people cannot agree on the meaning of innovation let alone what is innovative. What seems innovative to one person would seem pedestrian to another person.

Consider the simple example of the Segway. The Segway is a two-wheeled electric power transportation device that senses the user's weight shifts. It moves in the direction that the user shifts their weight. In reality the Segway is essentially an implementation of a classic control theory problem, the inverted pendulum. With built in motors and a clever control scheme, the Segway provides unique means of transportation. The user is able to move in almost any direction by simply leaning.

But, is the Segway innovative? It is built on a concept that has been around for a number of years in control theory. It has two wheels arranged in an unusual stance, sideways rather than front to back. And, it has incredible electronic controls and servo motor technology to produce its desired effect. In considering the Segway from an innovation point of view, you need to look at the component parts and consider if the device is itself innovative or are any of the components innovative? Maybe the combination of the devices yields an innovative mechanism. But, regardless of how innovation is defined, I personally had never seen such a device so it looked innovative to me at first glance. However, I was aware of the inverted pendulum problem in control theory so maybe the Segway was not innovative. I would consider the implementation of the Segway via its electronics to be very innovative. You can see the problem. Just what is innovative may depend on your background or your point of view.

To help us through this jungle, we will be looking at a model of innovation that will allow us to develop a context in which to evaluate innovation or claims of innovation.

CHAPTER 2

Concept of Innovation

One of the big questions I have puzzled over is the definition of innovation. This causes all kinds of gnashing of teeth and arguing during the product development process.

I want to use a simple definition of innovation: **"innovation is something that has not been done before."** Notice I didn't say useful because sometimes the product may be innovative but not useful. Sometimes innovation may be a perception of something new rather than anything that is actually new. But, at this stage let's just go with the simple definition.

There are large numbers of people who would not agree with that definition and we will discuss two categories of them and their reasoning.

First, and foremost, I seriously doubt that the US Patent Office would like my definition of innovation. The reason they would dislike my definition is that if I took two well-understood concepts and combined them, I could claim to have created an innovative product. The Patent Office would, under my definition, be deluged with inventions that were simple combinations of existing products and the entire system would collapse. But, how many products can you name that are really combinations of two very well-known products or variations on a combination of existing products. Reinvention of a product is innovation!

One of the key issues in this simple definition of innovation is that we live in a digital world. In such a world the general trend is that the semiconductor technology is constantly advancing and as the capabilities of the semiconductor chips increase the product designers are able to create more complex products. In this environment an obvious strategy is to add known functions (with some variation in the function's implementation) to an existing product. Thus, you actually end up building new (innovative?) products by essentially combining two or more existing products using a new design.

The second group that would have a serious concern about my definition is basic research scientists. There is a whole category of highly trained scientists who focus on the issue of trying to discover fundamental scientific capabilities. These people focus on the noble work of making basic scientific discoveries. They believe that they are able to find and assist others by developing new and innovative technologies. However, how many fundamental inventions do they really discover? And, are those inventions really useful, new and viable in an economic sense? How long does it take for their work to make an economic impact? Generally, they would view my strategy of reinvention to be of very low scientific merit. But they can never answer one question. If an "innovative" invention never leaves the laboratory and has no economic impact is it really innovative? This is the innovation equivalent of a tree falling in the woods.

In trying to define innovation and product innovation we need to deal with the issue of creativity. We are essentially trying to measure whether something is creative, innovative, unusual, new, etc. In many cases there are lots of ideas which can be viewed as an extension of other ideas or combinations of other ideas. The fundamental question is do we consider such ideas as creative? For our purposes we will take a very robust view of creativity. In the next section on products we will define a model of the innovative process that will allow us to examine a wide variety of concepts, products and companies.

If we are able to create an idea of a product then the challenge is to figure out if the product is innovative enough to stand out from the crowd of products or what needs to be done to make it stand out.

My bias is to try to develop products. The real measure of the importance of a technology is whether it can be used to create something that is new and useful.

Product development is very difficult because you are trying to develop products that are easy to manufacturer and at the same time have broad appeal. This is a very difficult balancing act. Success is elusive and difficult to obtain and maintain!

For our purposes we will talk about how to conceive and create new product ideas. But, we will use a very loose definition of what constitutes a product. Over time we will refine our definition as we talk about further details and concepts, but at this point in the book I want to use a simple definition of a product. That simple definition is "**a product is an item that we can sell.**" My view is that since technology allows us the ability to develop or evolve new products we want to concentrate our efforts on constructing concepts that we can sell. This is how we will define our concept of product. Our goal is to develop products that we can sell at a profit. At some point in time to accomplish our goal we may have to give some number of products away free to get the sales cycle moving forward.

From this foundation we will be able to extend and develop higher level structure. This will include sets of products, companies and even completely new abstractions that take over the consumer psyche to the extent that before the product was conceived people did not even know that they could not do without the product.

The process of creating categories of products that will obsolete other products we will call **creative disruption**.

CHAPTER 3

Concept of Reinvention

The key issue in developing products is how to get started. What is our creative strategy? If you can develop a basic concept you can then modify the concept and move forward. Lots of people have a lot of trouble getting off the ground. The key is to not let yourself get hung up by pebbles. Pebbles are small pieces of sand that seem to block people's paths and no progress is made. The worst thing that can happen when trying to move forward with a concept is to get stopped by a pebble. I do not care if you have a good or a bad concept. If you do not have a concept you will go nowhere. Thus, I will push for a concept regardless of the quality of the original concept. Why? Because I know that all concepts must have a lot of back and forth before they become viable and unless I have a starting point there will be no way to move forward.

The strategy that I wish to use is simple and is used by numerous people: reinvention. **Reinvention** is the process of taking as a basis a concept and then modifying the concept based upon insertion of new technology or processes. The probability of coming up with a truly useful and astounding radically new idea is small. Thus, I tend to want to conceptualize the design process as one of reinvention. (That is why the back cover contains a large set of quotes about reinvention by famous product developers.)

Reinvention is the key to creative disruption! A quality reinvention strategy equals creative disruption. Some critical quotes are provided below.

http://tinyurl.com/7wqhlp4

"Today Apple is going to reinvent the phone."
—Steve Jobs, Macworld Expo
January 9, 2007

http://tinyurl.com/7xyv9d7

"FORBES has been rigorously engaged in product reinvention over the last year."
—Lewis D'Vorkin, Forbes Magazine
November 21, 2011

http://tinyurl.com/7e589ru

"The Case for Product Reinvention-Product development at most companies is an evolutionary process, but some manufacturers have found the leap to an entirely new product line a profitable move."
—Jonathan Katz, IndustryWeek
Jan. 20, 2010

http://tinyurl.com/odgzxp

"In The Republic, Plato famously wrote, "Necessity is the mother of invention." What the esteemed Greek philosopher failed to mention is that reinvention is the way to build the mother of all companies."
—Patrick J. Sauer, Inc.
Apr 27, 2009

http://tinyurl.com/7wkrr7c

"The more important lesson is that anything that is invented can be reinvented and often should be since the original need, or problem, is still relevant."
—Max McKeown, Blog Post
May 24, 2011

CHAPTER 4

Problem of Venture Capital

The argument that I have used for reinvention over the years relates to VCs (Venture Capitalists). This is the VC conundrum. Once you have a real product concept, you may want to raise capital to get your company going and move that highly creative product to market. One way to accomplish raising capital is to go to a venture capitalist.

Consider innovation from the practical aspect of raising capital. Let's assume that you have no sales but you have a great business plan. Let's further assume that you have contacted a group of VCs who fund high risk start ups. (In the current economic climate finding such people is a miracle, but humor me for the moment.) At various points in my career I have worked for companies that are trying to raise capital and I have also been on the other side of the table working for the VCs evaluating business plans and proposed products.

The institutional process of VC investment requires that the VC do due diligence. Due diligence is the requirement that VCs figure out whether there will be a return on the money that they invest. It is a simple process. Is the management team capable and honest? Do they have a good idea? Is the amount of money being asked for reasonable? There is a series of such questions that must be answered. But, the key question for our discussion is, "What is the market and sales potential for the company?" We now can see the VC conundrum and the reasons for reinvention.

If you have a product that is so unique that no one has ever sold or seen such a product and it does not fit into any category of previously developed products, how can the VC figure out its sales potential? There is no way for the VC to figure out the potential and thus no way to complete the due diligence process. But, if the product is similar to existing products then the VC can make an estimate of market size based upon existing sales of similar products. It is that simple! Products evolve with simple incremental changes and this process of developing an innovative product starts with reinvention.

If you can create a massive change to the product and sales space you can create a disruption of the status quo. Our goal is to figure out how to create and quantify disruption. We will start with the idea of a concept and reinvention in the next part of the book.

Part I Conclusion

To begin our journey trying to create disruption in product sales status quo we will start with the initial step as product reinvention of a basic concept. We begin with simple definitions:

Innovation: innovation is something that has not been done before.

Product: a product is an item that we can sell.

Creative disruption: the process of creating products to obsolete other products.

Reinvention: the process of modifying an existing concept to produce a new product.

Our focus will be to conceive of products via a process that we will define as creative disruption—the act or process of upsetting the status quo by creating new products, companies or industries.

PART II

MODEL FOR DISRUPTION

In this part of the book, we examine how to use models to generate and measure creative disruption. We will see that the key to creative disruption in the product space is the concept of reinvention. Our model will provide us a vehicle to examine new concepts and a guide to their derivation via reinvention.

We will start with basic model structures: how to define, quantize and develop them and various strategies of creative disruption. We will end the discussion by looking at the parameters and directions such disruptions take us with a discussion of the parameters on our aspect directions.

The key point here is that a model can be developed that encompasses a variety of critical issues and that we can define components that will allow us to measure the potential for disruption caused by a technology or product. This model will start with a series of simple views or assertions about your product, customers and technology. In turn this will lead us to key questions regarding our product's placement strategy. From the overall model we can then determine if our product idea has the possibility of creating a region of disruption.

CHAPTER 5

Origin of the Model

For more years than I care to remember I have embraced the idea of developing a model of a product.

That's because I live and have lived in a world of chaos!

In one example I was involved in trying to take an existing product line and morph it into a new product line. The problem was that the company had a very large division with a viable product set that was under attack by other companies. These other companies had made a jump to new technologies that provided a competitive advantage over the company that employed me. I and a number of the top managers were tasked to figure out a new product strategy that would ensure the viability of the division. However, every time the group would meet, some minor nit would excite upper management and the group would go off in a new arbitrary direction.

It was truly amazing the lack of focus and understanding of the real issues.

If you cannot explain what your product is, does or might do, can you expect to explain to someone why they should buy your product? And, we are not just talking simple solutions. We are talking about any number of ways for customers to solve their problems. In other words, why do they need you?

Yet, one of the big complaints about models and modeling is that a model is not precise. It lacks fidelity. But, any model is better than the alternative, an explosion in a spaghetti factory. If you do not establish a model of your process, product or issue that you are trying to explore, you have no basis for making comparisons. In fact you have the real problem of letting some item that has no real impact get elevated to where it drives the decision process. And, the resulting decision is invariably wrong or irrelevant.

I am not trying to minimize the effort of building and understanding a model, but you need one to facilitate discussion. Thus, we will be building a model or innovation framework in this book. Not because it will be precise, but because it will be good enough for us to explain and explore alternatives of creating products. And it will allow us to understand the process of innovation and help us decide if we have been able to create a disruptive product. Remember in the product business good enough is good enough. Nothing is ever perfect!

There are a lot of different structures that can be used to develop a model: layered structure(s), wedding cake(s), globe(s), three dimensional Cartesian coordinate systems and graphs. These are just a few of the possibilities which I have used at various times. A subject as complex as innovation, and trying to create disruptive products, causes me to favor a model where we can single out key points in the process and in the spectrum of possible solutions. Further, I want the model to be able to delineate some number of views in this process. The process of developing a product is more art than science. We will be using a simple framework to deal with complex issues. We are looking at trade-offs rather than precise mathematics.

A good model to consider is that of a simple pie containing three "coordinates" as shown in **Figure 1**. This is our basic pie structure where the edges of a slice from the pie are an aspect of our problem solution. The center of the pie is our concept. We will be dealing with three sets of aspects and three questions along with our centerpiece, our concept. Each slice of the pie will also contain a question that we need to answer.

At this point we will begin defining the model we will be using for innovation.

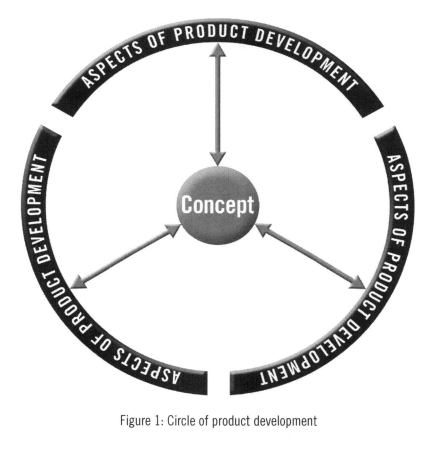

Figure 1: Circle of product development

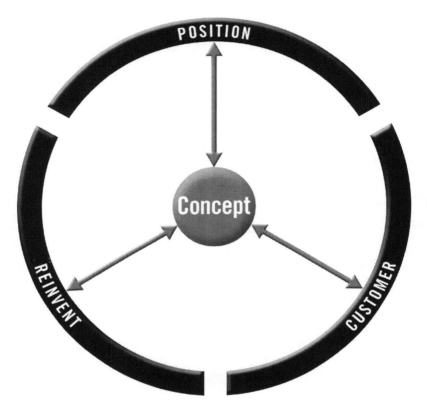

Figure 2: Elaboration on circle of product development

CHAPTER 6

Structure of Model

We begin with the idea of an axis taken from mathematical models. The axis usually represents variables that are independent of each other and can be mathematically related to each other. For our model of innovation (and the way that we can create a vision of disruption) that is a good feature. We will develop a set of reference points or axes that will allow us to define a set of functions. We will call those aspects. These functions will enable us to develop increasingly complex structures for our vision.

In our case, we will draw our model with ideas similar to the mathematical model, but instead of having axes, we will develop "aspects". Our model will contain three aspect sets of product development that we can examine and move our solutions along to ensure that we understand our product possibilities and position. Remember, the point at which the aspects come together is denoted as our concept.

The aspects are: reinvention, position and customer and are illustrated in **Figure 2**. Additionally, **Figure 2** lists the aspect values for each aspect that we will be examining and defining later in this part.

These are simple concepts that we will deal with in more

detail later, but the reasoning behind these choices is very simple.

Product reinvention is a strategy used by many developers who I know use to conceive of a product or its features. Various people define this in different ways: rethink, reinvent, refine, reincarnate, repurpose, etc. But, the basic idea is to conceive and implement a product based upon available technologies or perceived customer needs. This may not be philosophically satisfying. You might think that the great inventors are creating ideas out of thin air, but the reality is that the majority of great inventors are people who reinvent and repurpose. In a basic research lab that is not the case but we are talking about products and that's reality in the product world.

Product positioning involves defining what level of product you can build and where you can enter the market and the level of product that you can produce.

A product's customer is a realization that there are a variety of customers in the world. What you're trying to match is the customer, their sophistication, the size of the market and the positioning of the product.

We will deal with these issues in detail as we develop our model. **Figure 3** shows the complete model that will be presented in the next chapter.

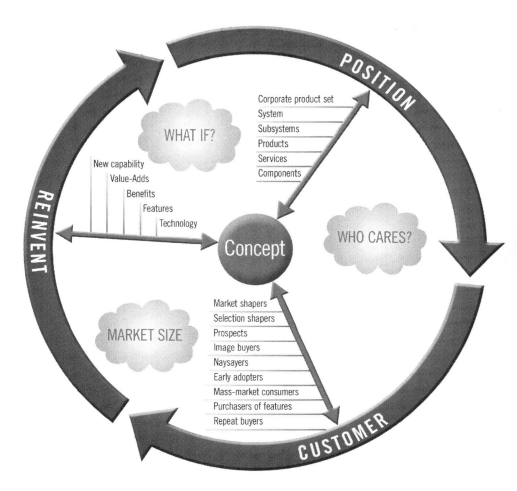

Figure 3: Structure of product development model

CHAPTER 7

Precision of Model

Unlike mathematical models that we may have encountered in our careers, our model will be pretty simple. The issue of creating a product and/or innovation is much like the process of making sausage. It is messy. Thus, although we will be using a pie slice system, the application of the process will not be simple. As we move further into the process of any aspect, the issues become more complex. As we move along an aspect from the concept we'll be able to see alternatives that are the properties of our product.

This process is imprecise and it's really more art than science. It is not scientific when you're trying to judge the effect of a decision and how it affects the product's position in the marketplace. Eventually, we will develop a set of relationships that will allow us to measure the product in terms of the level of sophistication that the product needs. It also allows us to measure how the product fits into the product space, who our potential customers are and how the product can evolve over time.

CHAPTER 8

Aspects of Innovation

Let's go back and review some of the ideas that were provided earlier in the book.

Innovation-**innovation is something that has not been done before**. In this case a product may be considered to be innovative if we combine elements that have not been combined in a particular form before. But, how innovative is that process? Therefore, we are trying not only to rethink a product but really extend a product concept and measure how the product fits into the product space.

Product-**a product is an item that we can sell**. We are trying to develop a product that not only can we sell but a product that has several advantages over products that might be considered somewhat similar. This provides us with a measure of how the product is positioned in the market and how purchasers may view our product.

We are trying to build a product that has the property of creative disruption so that we can achieve a high growth rate of sales. Our definition of creative, disruption and creative disruption are extended below with examples.

CREATIVE

1. ability or power to create

2. concept creation—creating instead of imitating

3. imaginative

4. avoiding conventional limitations

Use Examples

1. He came up with some *creative* ways to make money.

2. That is a *creative* solution to a difficult problem.

3. We can describe the first step in a *creative* process.

DISRUPTION

1. act of breaking apart or rupturing

2. act of interrupting continuity

3. a disorderly outburst

4. an event that causes discontinuity

5. the act of causing disorder

Use Examples

1. He created a disruption by interrupting the continuity of the presentation.

2. The disruption caused a break in the game's action.

3. Using a new technology they set in motion a complete change in the sales environment thereby causing massive disruption of the product sales channel.

Creative Disruption: the act or process of upsetting the status quo by creating a new product, company or industry

Use Example

1. Creative disruption caused the new technology of wireless networking to set in motion a new industry.

What I want our model to do, at a minimum, is to provide a means by which we can measure the excellence of our product against others, provide a framework to focus our thinking and lastly allow us to develop a product position plan and evolution strategy. Our product development strategy (creative, reinvent, position, disrupt) combines the goal of bounding reinvention and positioning with the act of creative disruption.

Using the strategy outlined below and derived from the model we do face a problem. We need to be very careful not to infringe on someone's patent, but this problem will be dealt with as we go through the creation and positioning process.

CHAPTER 9

Process of Creation

At this point I want to elaborate a little more on the creation process. In previous chapters I noted the ideas of rethink, reinvention, refine, reincarnate, repurpose, etc. In general, I have found that even looking at a product that people consider innovative, you can trace large parts of the product or its components back to products that you may have seen before. The best discussion that I have seen of this is in the context of the computer business where this process is called reincarnation (Figure 4, The wheel of reincarnation for input/output, page 7, *Computer Structures: Principles and Examples*, editors Daniel P. Siewiorek, C. Gordon Bell, and Allen Newell). In this description, the authors describe how reincarnation can be used to change the I/O of a potential computer system. Reinvention (and its related variations) have many references in the literature and seem to be a staple of inventors the world over.

The key to the computer industry is that the hardware technology is always changing and you can re-implement and combine functions or extend functions in creating a new product. Because patents tend to describe mechanisms and their implementations it is possible to get by with this strategy without infringing anyone's patent position. However, there is a large risk when you do this on a grand scale and you need to be very careful about applying the strategy that we are proposing without understanding your intellectual property rights.

But, in a majority of cases, product developers use a variation of the reinvent strategy to conceive of and develop a product. Product development is incremental, it does not move forward in large steps. The GLF (Great Leap Forward) of Chairman Mao was a failure and if you try to take too large of a step you risk failing miserably. Now some of my friends have said to me, that may all be true but how do you explain Apple? In response I ask, which product? In many cases I get back the response, the iPod. Well, not trying to cause Apple lovers to have heart failure, you could characterize the iPod as simply an electronic Walkman or Discman which Sony had developed years earlier. Actually, an aggressive product development student would say that the iPod wasn't even a knock-off of those products but instead it was an MP3 player with a clever interface and song distribution model. And, MP3 players were being sold by a variety of vendors before the iPod came on the scene.

In another view the iPod combined MP3 technology and created a song distribution method (iTunes). In that sense it's a product made by combining two known technologies or derivatives of two know technologies: MP3 players and peer-to-peer file sharing systems such as Napster. Where the MP3 players were a rethinking of Discman-like products which were a rethinking of Walkman-like products which were a rethinking of a cassette player on a boom box which were . . . In the case of Napster you could also make a similar lineage chart looking at incremental product improvements and history.

In looking closely at the iPod you will see that not only did Apple combine and reinvent several technologies, but they made it possible for you to store your own songs in iTunes. They also provided a very clever interface and display that made the device useable for an extremely wide class of user.

Simply said the overall iPod was reinvention product genius.

(Disclaimer—I own and use several Apple products including iPods, iPhones, and iPads.)

All that being said we should move along to a detailed discussion of the model.

CHAPTER 10

Features of Model

We begin by looking at our detailed model in **Figure 3**. Mathematical models have values that are noted on each axis. In our case we have aspects that are bounding our decision space or pie slice. These aspects are categories, not numbers, but the idea is the same. As we proceed out from the concept, the aspect values become more complex as our information becomes less precise and possibly more fluid. Oft-times we are unable to precisely delineate a boundary or the details that distinguish one concept from its nearest neighbor concept.

We start by examining our three product aspects. These aspects have been defined to let us discuss several key tradeoffs. All aspects attach to our concept and attempt to explain how our concept relates to the issues outlined for each aspect.

In the first case, we see the reinvent aspect. This aspect contains several values that drive the concept forward, allow us to reinvent the concept or provide guidance on how to modify (reinvent) the concept. The values we have available to us represent ways of looking at the process of reinvention: technology, features, benefits, value-adds and new capabilities. The further out we go from a simple technology, as the simplest form of reinvention, the fuzzier the process becomes. The easiest way is to take a concept and inject or modify technology and thus derive our new product or concept.

In the next case, we see the aspect of product position. This aspect contains a number of product or service concepts. For our purposes we'll stipulate that a service is as valuable as a product because we have a wide definition of a product. A product is something we can sell! We can sell services! We do not want our model or product to be limited to things that can be packaged up and carried out of a store. Thus, we have a simple definition and we try to be inclusive. We want to allow for a wide variety of product manifestations so that could mean anything from a haircut to a cup of coffee to a component for an airplane all the way to some combination of airplanes or computers. This aspect of our model starts with components, services, products, subsystems, systems, and finally goes to a corporate product set. A corporate product set is the most complex structure we will consider. The idea is that we need to move our concept into something we can describe and understand so we know how it fits against other products.

The last aspect in our model is the customer. In this aspect we are trying to measure or define who and what is our customer and what are their characteristics. In this case we are trying to distinguish between high volume customers and customers that are at the beginning of the adoption cycle. The values along this aspect are market shapers, selection shapers, prospects, image buyers, naysayers, early adopters, mass-market consumers, purchasers of features, and repeat buyers. For this aspect we are trying to define our potential customer base. This is particularly difficult over a wide set of potential products and potential marketing strategies. But what we must do is lay down a detailed set of expectations of who could be our actual customers and where we fit in the market spectrum. Clearly, the size of a market for a new product can be quite different depending on whether the product has mass appeal or is very special purpose. We need to measure this aspect. One of the easiest ways to measure is to think about what type of person would buy the product and where they fit in the product maturity spectrum. As a simple example, the customer who buys a notebook computer may be quite different from a customer who is in charge of buying a server farm. Lots of people buy notebooks, but few people buy server farms.

Our goal is to start with a concept and refine it by repetition of the tradeoffs defined by our slices of pie and bounded by our aspects.

Since we essentially have a simple pie-shaped model where each slice is bounded by two aspects, we can figure out some tests that we could perform on our concept. This allows us to measure more than one aspect. Consider the idea of looking at two aspects simultaneously. Because we have three independent aspects, we end up having three independent pie slices to consider. And, in a mathematical sense we can relate the aspects in the plane by a function. Since we are not trying to do this mathematically we are not really looking at a function of some precise variables. We will relate the aspects by critical questions that we will ask.

Consider the two aspects of product reinvention and product positioning. There really is a simple relationship between these two aspects. If we were to start with a simple concept and think about how we might change aspects by reinventing the product via the parameters we listed before, we can define a new product. The simple mapping of where the new product would end up on the product aspect line can be encapsulated by the mapping or question: What If?

A simple question, but quite profound!

If you are trying to develop a new product or concept, one of the easiest ways to think about the product is to take your concept, look at new technologies, features, etc. that you might add to your basic concept and then ask yourself "What If?" The answer to that question would take you to where your product firs in the product category and positioning aspect of the model.

You can move in both directions of the pie slice. You can move from reinvention to product and back again as you tune your concept and design. You must understand the concept of adjusting the design and altering the product's features. You need to constantly ask yourself what if.

What if? This will form our first and most basic question. Namely, can we define a product given a concept and a set of modifications of the basic idea?

The next mapping that we are interested in concerns the aspects of product positioning and customer positioning. Remember our basic notion is that a product is something that we can sell. If we wanted to give it away free then almost anything would be successful, but the trick is to find and identify the customers and potential users of the product so that we can sell the product. After all, our goal is creation and innovation and disruption of the status quo of similar products so that we can sell our product.

The basic question we need to answer when we define a product and we define a customer is "Who cares?"

I am not being heartless. Many people will say that if anyone stopped to consider their idea, they would immediately embrace the concept and buy the product. However, that is just not reality. You must position your product into a region of customer interest and then see how many people you can actually interest in your product. If you cannot articulate who would be interested in the product, you will never sell a single product!

There are a wide variety of customers and they have different interests and needs. But, most importantly, customers really are structured. For example, do you know the gadget guy? You know the person I am talking about. No matter what product has come into the market this is the person who has to have the latest and greatest gadget. The gadget may be expensive but he has it! This is the type of customer who was an early buyer of a 50 inch plasma high definition (hd) television. But more importantly before there was hdtv, there was edtv (enhanced-definition or extended-definition). And, you could spend 10,000 dollars buying a 50 inch plasma edtv. He did because from his perspective it was a must have and he had to have one to show off to his buddies. Once this set of early adoptors got the ball rolling, prices came down and the market took off. Eventually when the US government mandated a cutover to all digital programming, sales of hdtv spiked throughout the general population.

In terms of "Who cares?" we see a different set of potential customers resulting from the obvious cool factor to the real need of the customer to have and own a certain capability. Thus, in the aspect of customers, there is a broad range of customers that we can target and we need to understand when and where our product fits with these different types of customers.

The last question that we need to consider is "Market size?". It does not matter if we can answer the first two questions correctly if the market size for our product does not justify the investment needed to make it successful. Can we sell enough product at a high enough price to justify the investment? However, this is not a simple question because we do not expect that our first product will actually make money. The question is whether there is a scenario that over time will allow us to recoup our investment in the technology and make a profit.

Although it looks like we have simple questions and answers that will define our market, the problem we are dealing with is really both simple and very complex. It is simple in the sense we can estimate a market and draw an investment conclusion. It is very complex in that the simple analysis may not take into account all of the parameters that are in play as we begin to shake the product space.

We have no idea of the real market size until we commit to making our product and try to sell it. But, the idea is to use the "Market size?" question to try to measure our potential for product sales.

We are making more complex tradeoffs. We started with the idea of a simple pie slice model. We changed that into a model based upon aspects of product strategy and positioning. We started at our origin with a concept and aspects that reached out from that concept to describe reinvention, product position and product customers. We then developed three key questions in our model to allow us to critically think about the concept and its positioning and evolution. We now have three slices of the pie that we need to get into a position where they are in concert with each other if we are to be successful.

Clearly, everything is not precise as you might expect in a simple geometric model. We will discuss the need for iteration but for now we will drive forward with our model to examine another capability in this way of thinking.

Since the model is not precise mathematically, we will have degrees of "fuzziness." Let's first look at the aspect of reinvention. How precise is the difference in technology versus feature or feature versus benefit? We can go along any of our three aspects and we will find a blurring or lack of precision in the measures that are associated with our aspects. Is this a concern? If you expect that everything is precise, it would be. However, we all know that there are a lot of shades of gray or blending of concepts. This may make some people feel uneasy, but the reality is that everything is not always precise. To illustrate, consider a book on art history. In the book will be some "old master" paintings and there will be descriptions of the paintings that are quite factual. But, there will also be some verbiage about the meaning of the paintings. The painters died hundreds of years ago. How does anyone know what they intended or meant? In the same way, there is fuzziness in product conception, development and sales.

The model is not precise because it can't be precise. Some of the issues we are discussing are art. You need the model as a framework not as an absolute. It will never be precise, but it will be useful!

When considering a product, we need to keep in mind that we are really dealing with a fuzzy area on the aspect area of the model. For example, can you completely define and recognize an early adopter as opposed to a mass consumer? Yes, you can. However, trying to differentiate between customers that are closer to each other on the customer aspect of the model may be problematic.

We can build a further aspect of the model which is critical to us. This is the region of creative disruption. In this region we are trying to measure the product's overall potential based on all of the factors that we have considered. New Coke is an example of defining a completely new product with lots of studies showing what a success it would be and then being a complete failure. No one cared. Thus, we get the introduction (reintroduction of Coke) under the brand identity of Coke Classic. No matter how much effort you put into your plan you can still miss the mark. The region of creative disruption occurs when we get all of our questions answered and in concert so that we feel that the concept, positioning and customer base will allow us to create a disruption in the marketplace.

The region of creative disruption provides us with a basic overview of our product's potential position and potential for success.

Using our three aspect descriptions, three key questions and the region of creative disruption we now have product context and can compare it to its potential competitors. **Figure 3** provided the detailed overview of the model structure that we are using to frame future product reinvention strategies.

After creating our region of creative disruption you may think that our concept has moved along nicely. The reality is that we also need to develop a sense for the changes that may occur. We created our region of creative disruption assuming that all of our parameters will fall into place and the market is well behaved. It is not and never will be. Just as we had to understand that the aspects we look at may be fuzzy, we need to understand that the region is also fuzzy. It is also time sensitive. If we do not garner the resources to act, others may. Once we introduce our initial product, others will develop, reinvent and bring out their own products. The model we developed needs to undergo continual refinement, reexamination and modification. Repeat the analysis while refining it! Nothing in the world is static. Perceptions change and problems morph. We need to develop a set of models some of which are based upon technology maturity changes, some based on competitor reactions and some based upon future directions that we foresee. Even if we are not clear with our view of the future we need to use the model to try and foresee the pitfalls and our future. At a minimum we need to view the model as the first starting point. We may need to develop parallel models that reflect different functions we wish to introduce, competition possibilities and the aging of technologies that we chose for our product.

The three most important words in product reinvention: iterate, iterate and iterate! The alternative formulations are:

1. repeat the analysis, repeat the analysis and repeat the analysis!,

2. reinvent, reinvent and reinvent! and

3. refine, refine and refine!

You need to remember that you will probably not get the design correct in your first try so you will have to keep trying.

At any given point we will have a fuzzy feeling about where we are and the level of disruption that our new product may cause. We do not want to get too hung up on getting an exact measurement of the impact of our product as we begin to develop the concept. However, we need to understand that at some point we need to get a solid feel for the market size as our goal is to sell products. If there is no market, there is reason to develop the product! We will know the answer when we actually introduce a product and the market gives us sales feedback. But, in the meantime we need to refine our estimates and keep them realistic.

CHAPTER 11

Details and Definitions of Model

You must start with a concept no matter how simple it is. To get started just pick a concept. We need a simple concept. We could start with a product that we understand or some type of service. To make the discussion really simple we could start with something as simple as a general area in which we would like to work or create some type of product or service. It is not important that our starting point be detailed or has a level of sophistication. We just need a place to start. A simple example was Apple's reinvention of the smart phone. They started with the idea of reinventing a phone and then began to develop the product details. The concept was simple, a new type of phone. But the details must be worked out.

Many people find that attitude cavalier, but in the end I am looking for a solution and I will not get it in one pass. We must repeat the process! Thus, how far along my concept is at the start is not relevant. I will go through the drill and work through my framework. If I do not get as far along as I would like, I will use my result as the new concept and go through the framework again and again until I feel satisfied. I do not expect that I can go through this framework in one pass and get the final result. I constantly have to go through the exercise of positioning and refining my product.

Some people think that they should just be able to go through the exercise and the answer will be right there. That is just not possible in my experience.

View the process as a continuous process where you always have work to do. I want to think about the actual process like peeling an onion. Every time I take off a layer there is another possible layer to peel away.

Reinvention is the key starting point in our product development. Given any concept, we will use the idea of reinvention to hone and perfect the concept until it's fully developed. Sometimes we will want to start with an existing concept and evolve. Once we have a concept the process is to understand and position the concept until we can repeatedly develop a well-positioned concept.

We will look at aspects of reinvention. To do that we start near the concept and work our way out to the further reaches of the aspect.

Since I am inherently lazy, I will start with the simplest set of aspects. Also in some cases it may be difficult in product development to differentiate some aspects. But, humor me and believe that you can differentiate the concepts. We will be working with five aspects that I have found make reinvention easy to conceptualize: technology, features, benefits, value add and capabilities. These aspects are listed in **Figure 4**. Each will be examined briefly below.

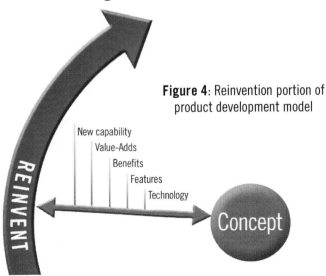

Figure 4: Reinvention portion of product development model

New capability
Value-Adds
Benefits
Features
Technology

REINVENT

Concept

Technology is the first aspect of reinvention that I like to use to define a product, concept or reinvention. The easiest way (subject to possible patent infringement lawsuits) is to take an existing product and build a knock-off using new technology. This is a time tested and proven strategy. You can not go wrong using this strategy! This is the process of reincarnation, reinvention, rethinking, reimaging, etc at its core. Just take an existing product and recreate it by inserting new technology or completely reinventing the product with new technology.

Features are another aspect. If a concept is new or very novel, you can always think of ways to add or delete features from the product or even describe the product by its features. If the product is not terribly sophisticated in terms of its capabilities, it is easy to select a set of features that will differentiate your concept from other concepts regardless of the underlying technology. Take an existing product or concept and vary its features. Feature modification gives us another time proven technique for (re)invention. As an example, consider the graphical user interface that Apple reinvented from the concepts created by Xerox which then were reinvented by Microsoft in its Windows operating systems.

As we move out further on the aspect of (re)invention, we encounter the dreams of marketing. We could approach the reinvention problem as a problem of user benefits. Can we describe our product in terms of how it benefits the user or customer? If we can, then can we think of benefits that distinguishes our product concept from other people's products? The value of discussing benefits is that we are able to drive home the concept of how we will create a benefit or solve a problem. This shows that we understand and can illustrate the ability to engage the user.

A further point in the aspect equation is the idea of value added. We are trying to describe not a benefit or technology or feature, but the ways in which our concept will bring some value to the customer or the customer's product experience. This is beyond the idea of a benefit. Our product will bring added value to the customer and the problem they are trying to solve.

As we near the end of the reinvention aspect we touch the issue of capabilities. At this point we may be able to do something that is truly new. We are bringing a new capability that the customer has not seen before. If we can do this then we have built the unique product, the "wow" product. But, it is really very difficult to create a "wow" product (one that we have truly not seen before) that defines a new product category.

We will start with the aspects of products and product positioning summarized in **Figure 5**. Again we start near the concept and work our way out to complex structures. This area will be a little more complex as we would like to cover both manufactured and service based products, so at least one transition will be quite fuzzy.

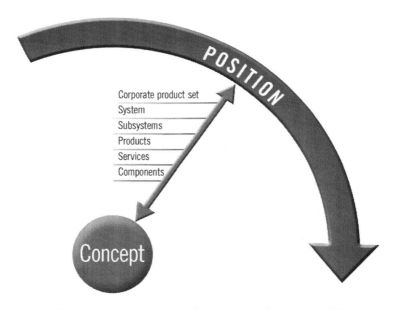

Figure 5: Position portion of product development model

We start with the idea of a component. Generally, you are not able to conceive or develop a full product on your first try. Although, given an initial product you can usually build a new version and with repeated iterations you can develop a new product. In many cases the initial product that is developed is a component. This may be a complex component such as a computer or something as simple as a fastener. But this is the lowest level of a product that we can sell. Generally it will need to be integrated with something else to provide value. By itself it's incomplete but it becomes very useful when combined with other components.

Above the idea of a component we have two ideas: a service and a base product. Remember a service can be as valuable as a product. A service is something that we sell that may or may not involve the sale of a physical item. In our product aspect we are looking to sell a service or a commodity that we can deliver but it may not involve delivery of tangible assets except to the purchaser. An example of a service is a haircut (and not the Wall Street version of a haircut). We can build a business around the basic concept of a haircut.

A product by our definition is something physical and tangible that we deliver that provides a stand-alone value. It may be further enhanced by the addition of components.

As we climb further along the product aspect we will encounter a subsystem. Subsystems are generally composed of multiple integrated products that form a major function in a larger context. An example of a subsystem (in the software sense) is Microsoft Word.

Systems are at the top of the product food chain and they may be complex, highly integrated products, such as an application running on top of a server farm driving a business application like order entry. Alternatively, the system may be a cup of coffee served by a coffee shop as that cup of coffee is probably the top of their product line.

Corporate product sets consist of a series of products designed to provide the customer with a variety of the company's choices of basic and extended products. Generally such products are set up to provide a set of options in price and capability to ensure that customers spend their money at your location.

Given a product concept, we can articulate where we think it fits from the aspects of reinvention and product position. Then we need to think about how it fits in the market. The further out conceptually the product seems the more difficulty we will have trying to determine where and how the product fits into the spectrum of available products.

A difficulty with customer aspects is that we need to think about how and where the product fits into the customer base. In many cases, we may not have a good feel for how the product can be positioned. Sometimes people will misunderstand this problem and look at their product as being extremely unique to the point that they view the product as having no competition. Every product has competition. Even if the product does not have a direct competitor, it will have products that are in adjacent market spaces. Because of this fact, you can conclude that every product has competition. In the sense that there is a fixed amount of money available in the world to buy products, every product has to compete for its share of that money. The lack of a direct competitor does not mean lack of competition. Product customer aspect analysis is very difficult. It requires extensive experience and practice. **Figure 6** summarizes the customer aspects of our model.

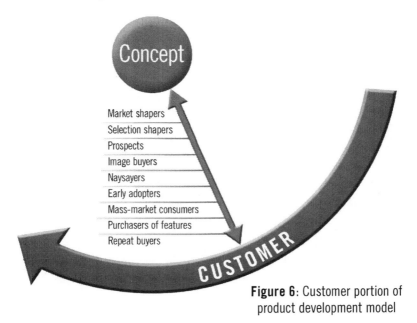

Figure 6: Customer portion of product development model

We will start this aspect of analysis with a very limited view by considering the issue of market shaping. How do we relate to a very small group of potential customers—customers that we can reach by trying to develop a position or shape of the product market. In this aspect we are just running tests to see what the market might look like under certain conditions. Is the product so special purpose that each sale must be shaped individually? That is the key question at this point.

Selection criteria analysis involves performing analysis about what causes the customer to consider purchasing the product. What is the aspect or issue that would cause the customer to become enamored enough with the product to actually purchase the product? Are there similar products? Is there an aspect of the reinvention that we can use to make the product attractive to customers who are out looking to purchase a product that meets specific criteria? In this case the product sale is involved with a limited and select number of customers.

If we have developed a product that has a wide range of uses or potential customers, we can begin to look for customers in a broad spectrum of areas. This is the aspect of a product that has a wide customer base so we can begin prospecting for customers on a wider base. The question now is can we make the product so it has appeal and potential to grow into a consumer product?

Image development is the next customer aspect. In this aspect we are trying to position the product in such a way that the customer will achieve a level of cachet that comes with being the owner of a unique and scarce product. This stage of product aspect still does not involve mass consumer product sales but may involve tailoring of the product to specific affinity groups.

Naysayers comprise the group of potential customers who will always find something wrong about the product. They are similar to people who never think anything is innovative or can always find fault. At some point you must get your product past this group or you will never be able to get large-scale product sales.

Once we have a scarce but standard product ready for mass

distribution we arrive at the aspect point of customers known as early adopters. Early adopters are consumers who are the early buyers of high volume products. They are important because if you can get them on board, they will create the buzz that will drive your product forward. It is critical to get early adopters on board because buzz can cause the phenomenon that we see when Apple or Microsoft bring out a new product; people line up all night to be the first to get the new product. Early adopters make or break a product as they determine if a product moves into the mass market.

Mass market products are the gold standard for product sales. These are products that are bought in large quantities and are ubiquitous in society. This is where we want to get our product positioned. Large volume and big brand identification are key to large scale product sales.

Ilities are a way of describing product features. Some buyers buy on the basis of features alone. Within the context of systems engineering, quality attributes are non-functional requirements used to evaluate the performance of a system. These characteristics are sometimes named "ilities" after the suffix many of the words share. For example, a product may be scalable (possess the property of scalability) or it may be extensible (possesses the property of extensibility). Ilities are ways of extending a product concept that gives your mass market purchasers a way to justify that your product is better than comparable products. Ilities are difficult concepts but users of products seem to dote on them. People generally use them as nouns; they may actually be adjectives or verbs if supported properly. Scalability is a difficult concept to fully grasp. It is better to describe system architecture as being a scalable architecture if it is supported by tradeoffs and explanations. To be scalable is also acceptable if supported by how the concept is applied. A simple example of this is game consoles where you can buy more games; i.e., extends the game console by adding to the product. In this category you can foresee sales developing due to add-ons to existing high volume products.

Customer care for repeat customers is the final area of

customer aspects in the sense that once we have a product set with an installed product base we not only can sell new product, but add-ons and service. In this category we want to keep our existing customers while stealing other customers by enhancing our image either in a product or corporate sense.

Unlike a mathematical model which can usually be described with a precise model, the aspect product has a large amount of ambiguity! If it were precise then anyone could perform the product definition. You should not be concerned about ambiguity and difficulty of use. This basic strategy has served me for a large number of years and allows for the successful definition of products from a functional and customer position. There are, however, some key issues that need to be addressed in using such a model.

First, not everyone is equally skilled and can grasp the strategy put in play by using this model. Generally, the first time you try to define a product it will be very difficult, but if you can arrange your thinking into the framework described, you will be able to successfully describe and conceive of products.

Second, even if you are not able to synthesize products, the model will provide you a framework with which to compare other people's products. This is useful especially if you are in the marketing and sales departments of a company. You need a way to consistently view competitive products and try to figure out what their key capabilities, deficiencies, vulnerabilities and issues are.

Third, the adjacent concepts on any given aspect originating from the product concept you are considering may not seem to have a lot of differentiation, but as you move out the aspect direction, there are a lot of differences in the basic aspect concepts.

Fourth, a product may not have a precise position on a given aspect direction. It may cover a couple of concepts on the aspect. This will allow you to see how different products will be viewed in many different ways from a strategic viewpoint.

Lastly, when you look at the areas of disruption that we set up, you need to note that there is another dimension not shown in the actual model. This is the dimension of time. When you make a pass through the model and develop a product concept and positioning, you are just making an analysis at a point in time and you may have to go through a periodic review of the model and your product position as time and technology change.

Mathematical models can be very precise. The described aspect model needs to be considered from the start as a fuzzy model that tries to illuminate issues that are keys in describing aspects of a product and its potential customer set. But, you should not expect it to be precise. It is important to understand that there will be fuzzy concepts that you are dealing with at any point in time.

We need to understand this key model mechanism. Product conception and development is not a precise science. It is art and you need to learn to think of products in a relative structure comparing their relative positions on key issues. But you can never get a completely direct and precise comparison of two products let alone two corporate strategies.

Further, even two closely related products and companies will differ, at least in their customer acceptance. Their product and corporate positions will not be similar. It is possible over time for one company (that is behind another company in terms of customer acceptance) to be able to see how the companies and their product positions differ and to begin to adjust their strategies. If they have staying power the company starting from behind may be able to reposition itself to become the market leader.

In thinking of how to use this model, you need to understand that it will work in an iterative fashion. You should not assume that you can just make one pass from concept to reinvention and expect that you have a new product concept that will find customer acceptance.

The way to use the model is to start with a concept, consider ways to reinvent the concept, try to define the concept and understand its market position. You do not necessarily end up with a viable product by just performing the basic steps. If you do not have a viable concept then you need to repeat the process by taking what you think works in the reinvented product and reinvent it again.

After several tries you should converge on a product that is well enough positioned and defined that you can make solid market estimates.

At this point you will have to adjust the product definition to ensure that you have a product that has a viable market. This may again require repetition of the process.

Multiple tries through the model should give you a clear understanding of the quality of the basic idea and whether there is a market path that can result in a viable profitable product.

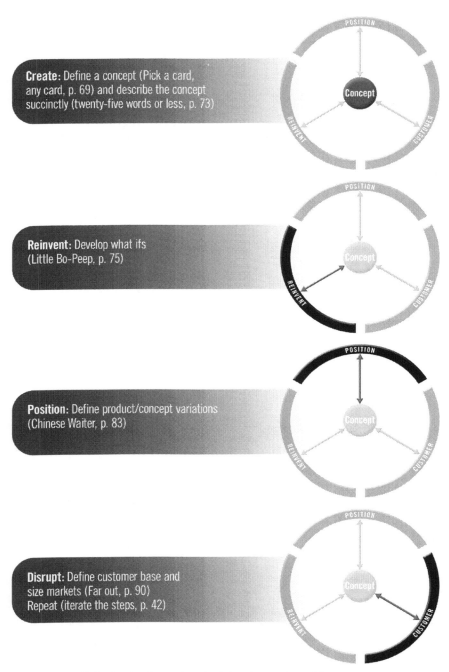

Create: Define a concept (Pick a card, any card, p. 69) and describe the concept succinctly (twenty-five words or less, p. 73)

Reinvent: Develop what ifs (Little Bo-Peep, p. 75)

Position: Define product/concept variations (Chinese Waiter, p. 83)

Disrupt: Define customer base and size markets (Far out, p. 90) Repeat (iterate the steps, p. 42)

Figure 7: Cyclical nature of product development model

CHAPTER 12

Three Key Questions Driving Model Use

Once we have the basic model structure and the aspects of our product space, we can begin to think of how to use the model in abstract terms. We want and need to make the model dynamic. We want to relate the different aspects and begin to understand how to create and modify our product in terms of its feasibility and usefulness. We will need to understand how the product and its variations can be sold to real customers and thus move out of our imagination and into the mainstream of product sales.

To understand how to use the model we need to consider three questions: What If? Who Cares? Market Size? These questions are our starting point to the reinvention space. From there we can build scenarios and product positions that reflect our analysis of what a product could or should look like to sell to different user categories. These questions are summarized in **Figure 7**. We examine each of these questions below.

What If? relates the ideas of reinvention and position.

"What If?" is our starting point for reinvention. If we have a concept (of any quality or depth of description) we can begin to modify, complete or enhance the concept. This is done by looking at the product and adding or subtracting from the product concept reinvention aspects that we have previously discussed in our model. This sounds like an easy task, but it is actually quite difficult. We need to build a complete description of the new concept and in that process we need to think about and enumerate all of the details that we expect to have in the new product concept.

One of the difficulties of performing the task of reinvention is that we need a strong leader or a really small team to accomplish the task of looking and thinking about reinvention aspects and using the what if proposition to move our concept onto the product aspect. This is the time that we can get bogged down by pebbles. Pebbles are small issues that involve details below the level of product definition that will cause us to lose the focus of the total picture. A pebble that could be encountered is a designer's favorite hot button. If the designer feels comfortable with a feature they may always try to add it to the product. It is important to try to develop the concept to a consistent level so that we can actually evaluate the probability and cost of a product implementation. For now we will assume that we can solve these issues.

The "what if?" question will allow us to move from concept to product and then into a product category. Basically, we start with a concept and a category of ideas to focus our reinvention strategy to get us to where this reinvented concept fits into a product aspect.

This is the easiest part of the process. Lots of people can come up with the what if aspects, but very few people can move up to a consistent product aspect position as they tend to get sidetracked and don't get beyond the myriad possible reinvention aspects. It will take a strong leader to create a concept that we can examine in the sense of a positioned product.

In the next part of the book, ideas will be provided to assist you in making the leap from the reinvention aspect to the product aspect via the what if question.

Who Cares? relates the product to the customer.

Who cares is the second question but it is also a really tough question. As we progress thorough our three questions each question becomes more difficult to answer and requires more honesty and self-examination. Are we really providing a product that someone would actually buy or is it just a figment of our imagination?

Every designer thinks that the world will beat a path to their door and they will sell lots of products. Someone beating a path to your door is really a fairy tale. Lots of ideas just go into the trash bin. Just because you can describe a product that somehow is different, unique or in your mind special, does not mean that anyone cares.

This is the really difficult part. You need to come to grips with the realities of whether there is a customer who will care about your product. The more radical your product, the more work you have to do to determine whether anyone actually cares. The answer to this question is really difficult as everyone wants to think that their product is important and would be well received. But this is usually not the case—like the proud parents who believe that their baby is cute. In reality most babies are not cute, but people with ugly babies find it difficult to come to grips with that fact. Likewise, if you design a product you are invested in the process. You think it's important but no one may really care about the product.

The answer to this question will require some deep introspection and serious analysis to figure out where is the market space for your product.

Market Size? relates market size and reinvention because you not only need a viable market and product but you must generate a market large enough to make it worthwhile to build and sell the product.

Market size is a complex question. It's dependent not only on whether anyone cares, but is also highly sensitive to competition (or potential competition) as well as pricing. There are clear relationships between whether anyone needs your product and its cost. It is not just an issue of whether we are able to create a new product that people care about but whether we can create a value proposition that makes the potential customer actually buy the product.

The market for a product can be highly varied. If you are selling a refueling tanker to the US Air Force, you can focus your efforts on what the customer thinks the market size is; they will tell you how many tankers that they intend to buy and when they will buy them. On the other hand, if you are in the business of selling coffee to people who walk by your store during specified hours you will not have a lot of insight into the number of cups you will sell other than trying to determine the number of people walking by your store.

Determining the market size in the coffee case illustrates the potential complexity of the process. First, there is the issue of the amount of foot traffic going by the location. Then, there is the issue of whether there are other shops nearby selling similar products. And then what happens to weekday traffic versus traffic on holidays and weekends? So it can be tricky to determine how to capture a percentage of the traffic going by on any given day and time period. This involves a complex market analysis. You need to think about what you can do to create a sense of urgency in the potential customers to get them into your shop.

The more complex your product and the more familiar the potential customer is with your product, the more difficult it is to size your market. You need to think in terms of segmenting your potential customers and thinking of ways to entice portions of the customer base to buy. Only then can you build an estimate of your sales.

The techniques described above generally fall into the category of market research—not an exact science. What causes one computer company, one coffee company or one hamburger franchise to dominate is the subject of mystery. It involves not only product positioning and good technology and products but also luck and vision. We are only examining how to get our product conceived and positioned in this book. There are a wide variety of books that purport to teach you how to actually sell the product and build the next Apple, Starbucks or McDonald's. Once you have created your disruption you need to consult books on how to build that next great company.

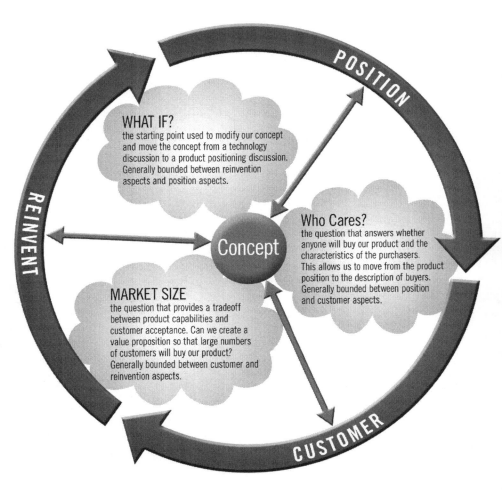

Figure 8: Elaboration on questions

CHAPTER 13

Creative Disruption Using Model

By thinking about the process of product development we can develop a product scenario that describes our product. By this I mean that we can build a process that allows us to describe and conceive of our product and how it relates to extant products. It also shows us how to reinvent or position ourselves against such products, what is the actual product and its position in a spectrum of product possibilities. And, most importantly, how we can sell our product to customers is addressed throughout our development process. **Figure 8** summarizes the overall strategy.

During this process we need to answer some serious questions. The most difficult of which is the question of whether anyone really cares about our product vision. Do not be deceived into thinking that this is a simple question. We will find incredible inertia and defensiveness in the process of trying to determine whether anyone really cares. Everyone wants to think that someone will care about their idea. The question of whether anyone really cares will encounter incredible resistance and comments about how things ought or should be as no inventor wants to hear that no one cares about their idea.

One of the key issues that you must deal with is how many people really care about your product or idea. Focusing on the issue of how to position and the potential customer base is designed to address this key question in a rational fact-based non-emotional manner (at least to the level we can ascertain facts).

CHAPTER 14

Space of Disruption

Once we have created our disruption, now we face several real challenges. One of the challenges is that nothing is static. We've really defined our space of creative disruption once we've run through all the potential issues and we've gotten our disruption to where we feel comfortable with all aspects of the product. This space is bounded by our idea of reinvention, our definition of the product and our positioning of the product. We have now defined the space in which we intend to operate and have answers to the three key questions.

The last thing that we need to understand is that we are dealing with a dynamic concept. As time goes on, the region that we have defined as our strategic disruption as well as the answers to our key questions change. That is, the region changes over time due to changes we make or competitive changes in the market place. When we defined the product, we set it up against a set of criteria. Technologies and time will change everything.

You need to constantly reexamine your creative disruption to see how it needs to evolve as the world evolves. You cannot view this process as static.

Part II Conclusion

In this part we have discussed the idea of models that let you develop knowledge about a product and how to apply the model to understand relationships and aspects that you need to consider developing and positioning a successful product that will create a marketplace disruption. We have developed a simple model of the aspects of product concepts that we need to describe and conceive of products that have the potential to be disruptive. What we are trying to do is to develop measures and ways to describe products that will enable us to distinguish between pebbles and the Matterhorn!

This is not the only way to approach this problem; however, this is a way that I have used for years and it can and will work for you. It is important to remember that you will have to make multiple passes through the model and you cannot let your ego get invested in your solution. There is no real "right" answer! There is today's correct answer which may not be correct tomorrow. Lastly, the results that you come up with are really more of an application of art rather than science. And the "result" is not a static region of creative disruption but a region that will constantly change based upon unforeseen future events and evolution.

PART III

APPLICATION OF CONCEPTS

In this part, we examine ways to move forward to ensure that we can develop creative disruption. We believe that the key to creative disruption is the concept of reinvention. But actually moving forward can be a problem. Our model provides us a vehicle to examine new concepts and a guide to their derivation via reinvention. But we need techniques to frame and make decisions. Such techniques are what we will discuss here.

We begin by looking at how we view our basic model structure. Then, we examine techniques that enable use of our basic model structures. Next we want to define, quantize and develop the region of creative disruption contained within the model. We want to end with a discussion of the parameters on our aspect directions.

The key point is that we can use simple techniques that will allow us to move through the processes to create strategic disruptions.

The simplest and easiest way to accomplish reinvention is to start with a concept. In a sense it is like a card trick—pick a card any card. Well, almost any card as the degree of difficulty of our problem is lessened if we pick intelligently. Then the trick is to move the concepts out of reinvention and group them into categories based upon how complex and related they are. At this point you have a set of possibilities that you can use to define your product.

Then, you make a set of product definitions based upon the what if possibilities which in turn allow you to generate product(s) concept(s). Next you run trial product concepts into market analysis so you can determine the size of the market. At this point you should have a reasonable product and begin more detailed designs. If you do not have a solution that is converging or is too abstract, you begin again using the completed concept as our new starting point. After a set of iterations, you should converge on a viable concept.

Our model is reprinted in **Figure 9**.

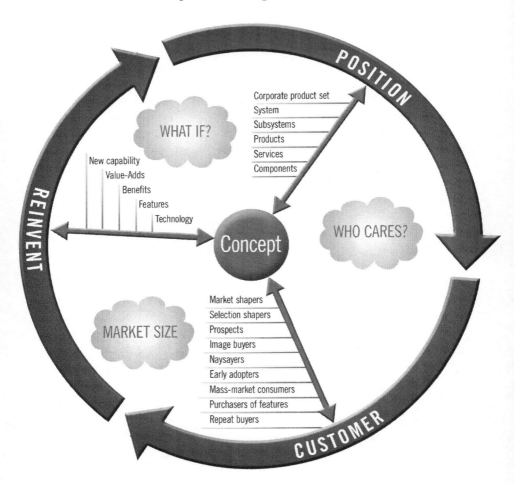

Figure 9: Structure of product development model

CHAPTER 15

Pebbles and Solutions of Development

Pick a card, any card! What about this problem? Here is another problem. Consider this problem.

One of the big problems is pebbles!

There are tons of problems in reinventing products, but the big problem is that of inertia. You can get bogged down in minutiae. And, you have no way to get the process moving forward with a degree of expediency. My solution to this problem over the years has been to use humor that has real points, keeps things moving and keeps everyone from getting irritated. Some of these solutions and analogies are a little unconventional but they work. They will be the subject of the remainder of this chapter.

I have used this basic model structure in various forms for years. Over the years, it has gotten more sophisticated and complicated. Yet, using it is pretty simple. However, I understand that there is a big gulf between telling someone about the model, showing them how to use the model and then actually having that person successfully apply the ideas contained in the model. The fact that I can use the model and apply its techniques does not mean that others can. Whether any individual can actually perform a task given an example is the real question.

As I have indicated, this is not the only way solve the problem. I have seen other approaches and tried to incorporate their ideas into mine. In fact, it is only recently that I have tried to describe to others how I actually go about this process. I am in a position where it is incumbent upon me to ensure the success of a large number of people trying to develop new technology concepts. Recently, with the economy mired in trouble and the jobs that we are trying to perform becoming very competitive, I have been trying to get a large part of my staff into position to provide a consistently high level of performance. Thus, I have actually documented how I go about approaching the problem.

It is important that my staff be successful. It is important that they not waste time and energy on techniques that do not produce results. In that vein, I have adopted a strategy where I try to show them by example and suggest various ways to improve their performance. To this end, I have become motivated to write down a practical working strategy that can be generally applied.

The strategy that we will apply consists of the previously described model and ways to keep ourselves on track as we try to use the model. These techniques are designed to keep us moving and are discussed in this chapter.

This brings us to the subject of pebbles. The key to developing a product is: don't let pebbles stop you from moving forward on any aspect of product development. You must start somewhere. Pick a solution and iterate. That being said, pebbles, or the perception of a pebble, are the major difference between a successful and unsuccessful product developer. It is the ability of developers to understand that they cannot have all of the answers at the start of the project and that there are some issues that will just have to be dealt with later that distinguishes successful developers from unsuccessful developers.

In many cases you will read about successful product developers and you will hear how abrasive and difficult they are to get along with. Another way to look at this is that they are really focused on getting the job done and they do not have time to deal with superficial issues. In my experience, a successful developer has a focus on the development to the exclusion of all other issues. A drive to complete the product knowing that the product will not be perfect, but can be successful is the key.

Along the way there will always be an issue that you cannot anticipate and you must move on.

Pebbles are incidental issues that will cause you to drill down to solve the issue but stop you from moving the product to completion. If you could solve every pebble you would have a perfect product, but it would never be complete because it would never be perfect.

It is important to keep your product definition moving forward. Periodically, you will encounter issues that you missed or had not considered. When this occurs you must decide if they are really important issues or if they are pebbles. Pebbles are really issues that you do not need to consider right now. As such you should put them onto a list for later consideration or go back through the model taking into account their importance and impact. Our goal should be to develop a set of product descriptions that gets the key issues settled first. We can then keep drilling down into the product description making the product definition more detailed each time we go through a product iteration. Our goal is not to fixate on a particular feature and drill down to solve that feature to the exclusion of all others. We are looking for a balanced approach and a consistent level of definition of the product.

We must make sure that we have a balanced approach to the product definition.

I do not mean to over emphasize the issue of pebbles, but it this singular focus of solving the big picture issues and continuing to refine the product structure that separates the accomplished designers from the also-rans. Dealing with a large population of highly educated people I have tried to instill this type of thinking into the process. It has yielded a variety of results. Some people approach the problem and adopt the model because it is similar to the way that they were addressing the problem to begin with. Other people have no clue and after multiple attempts to assist them I have given up in a number of cases because it is clear that they may never really be able to perform at the level they need to be successful.

However, there are techniques that if they were to embrace would further assist them to be successful. In some cases there is no hope for some people to actually be successful and we need to recognize them for their other skills. Thus, in the rest of this chapter I will give you some crutches that I have used over the years to help you in your journey and process as you try to understand how to develop products.

We begin with trying to develop a focus!

CHAPTER 16

Product Focus of Model

At the core of our model is our concept or product. This is the basis on which we are trying to develop our product and to position ourselves in the market. It is from this beginning that we will start our process and develop the description of what we hope will be a disruption of the status quo.

If we accept the VC conundrum (that we previously discussed in Chapter 4) and the idea of reinvention, we have some point of product description to begin our journey. It is important that this description or concept be very well defined. It is important that we get a good foundation.

For the foundation, I would like to use a simple principle. I wish to be able to describe the basis of the product and its relationship to the current state of the art in twenty-five words or less!

When I was growing up it was common for companies to run contests where they wanted you to articulate why you bought their product in twenty-five words or less. Even though I was not a good writer, I tried to enter these contest as often as possible. I never won any of the contests that I entered! But, I was always trying. In retrospect, such contests are not much different from the concept of the elevator speech that you must be able to articulate to an investor if you are trying to raise money for a new product concept; or the simple pitch that a sales person would provide to a potential customer to close a sale.

I want to start the product development with a simple statement of what it is that the product has to do. I want that statement to be twenty-five words or less. I want focus on what we are trying to accomplish. I want focus on where we are trying to go. I want focus on our competition, but I want a focus that is understandable and concise. I do not want an explosion of ideas in a spaghetti factory that will cause me to waste time on pebbles and spaghetti fragments that are going off all around me.

An alternative formulation of this strategy is the "famous" bar napkin design process. In many cases designs have been laid out on bar napkins and entire companies founded around such processes. Again, because of the limited space on the bar napkin you end up creating a really focused proposition about the product, its features and how you can structure the market position of the product.

It would seem to be a simple exercise to be able to describe a product or a concept in twenty-five words or less, but it is really hard. You hear stories of product concepts that were originally developed and described on bar napkins, but the napkin design strategy is difficult. It is very difficult to succinctly describe a product or concept. When people try to perform this task, they invariably end up diving down to issues that are not relevant or getting side tracked on an issue that does not impact the overall result. It takes practice to actually perform this simple description.

In one sense we are trying to describe the first order effects of the product. This is difficult because it is human nature to try to describe a product in terms of other products that are familiar. In many cases, this tendency takes the description in a direction that involves the details of a product and not its concept. One needs to be careful to try to describe what it is that the product does, not how it actually functions. Once you begin this description you should focus on only one facet of the product.

It may seem easy but you need to try to describe a product or concept in twenty-five words or less. In the next chapter we will talk about the ditty, "Little Bo-Peep." It has only twenty-five words. And, it can be described easily in twenty-five words or less by simply stating it is "a ditty about a little girl with sheep."

CHAPTER 17

Question of "What if?"

Once we have a concept we will need to see if we can figure out how to move forward. This involves moving out on the reinvention aspects of the product and developing more product details by adding at least one aspect of product redefinition to the base concept. Once we have gone through a complete cycle of definition or reinvention we may choose to add further product aspects. As we perform this exercise we constantly need to ask ourselves what if. By constantly reexamining and reinventing our product concept we can begin to get the product into a better defined form. Eventually we get the product defined to the point we can actually build the product.

This is not easy.

Avoiding pebbles and thinking outside the box is the key at this point. And, we have to avoid getting stopped until we have brought the design to the next level. Pebbles abound in my world. I think that one of the best ways to break up or sweep away a pebble is with a hint, crutch, humor or process work around. In the previous chapter I suggested focusing on the idea of writing the basic concept in twenty-five words or less. In this chapter I suggest that you use an old comedy shtick.

When I was growing up in the 50s there was this comedy routine that I found quite funny. It is called, "It's in the book," by Johnny Standley, and today it can be found on youtube.com at **http://tinyurl.com/2vw3bd6**. Additionally, the song can be heard playing in the final scene of the movie The Last Picture Show. In this routine which is a parody of the 50's and 60's television evangelists (at the time they were considered wild and crazy guys and the shows were pretty wild, but in today's context they would be considered tame), there are two parts. In part one the subject is Little Bo-Peep and her lost sheep. This is the part of the routine that is of interest to us.

As I was working in my career, I spent a considerable amount of time in meetings with others trying to develop concepts for new products and how they fit into the market. Not only was it difficult to keep the discussions on track but often the suggestions and ideas pursued by the participants were so crazy that one of the ways I thought about the problems at hand was to think about Little Bo-Peep and her lost sheep. Eventually this process became a staple of mine when trying to get people to think outside the box or to consider alternative approaches to design issues. It also provided me comic relief when I was faced with people who just tried to make a pebble into the Matterhorn and we could not get them to budge or move forward in any fashion.

Consider the basic verse of the tale:

Little Bo-Peep has lost her sheep,
And doesn't know where to find them;
Leave them alone, And they'll come home,
Wagging their tails behind them.

There are variations and additional verses that you can find, but this is the way I learned it.

In his routine, Standley goes about analyzing the poem noting (and I have left out parts to simplify the initial discussion):

"it's reasonable to assume if Little Bo Peep had lost her sheep, it's only *natural* that she wouldn't know where to find them.

That, basically is reasonable, but, uh, "leave them alone." . . . Think! If the sheep were lost, and you couldn't find them, you'd have to leave them alone, wouldn't you?

"Leave them alone and they"—they being the sheep—"they will come home."

"They will come home . . . a-waggin' their tails . . . ." Pray tell me what else *could* they wag? "They will come home a-waggin' their tails behind them . . . *behind* them!" Did we think they'd wag them in front? Of course, they might have come home in reverse."

In this case this is a great example (and if you have a sense of the absurd it is very funny) of trying to think out of the box. Standley comes up with a couple of funny ideas. One is if she lost the sheep she would not know where to find them. Two is if she leaves them alone they will come home. Three is that they will wag their tails behind them unless they come home backwards.

If we are trying to think out of the box we need to think about three critical issues. I will give you some simple examples but you will be able to think of a lot of alternatives once you seriously think about the simple rhyme.

First, we need to question what we know. Two we need to think about alternatives. And, three we need to make up lists of possible solutions knowing that we may never be able to solve the problem completely.

If we look at the nursery rhyme about Little Bo-Peep, in the category of what we know, do we really know anything about Little Bo-Peep? For example: 1—is there really a Little Bo-Peep? 2—does she have sheep? 3—has she lost them? 4—do we have any reason to think that they may come home? 5—do sheep wag their tails when they walk? 6—can sheep walk backwards? We can generate a whole list of questions (or what ifs) based upon examining what we do or do not know about the information that we have been presented. The above set of questions is simply a small subset of the questions we can ask if we question what we know.

Then we can think of generating alternatives to the questions. For each question there can be a set of alternative questions that we need to examine. Let's assume that there is a Little Bo-Peep. For example, for the question of whether she has sheep (question 2 in the above paragraph): 1—where did the sheep come from? 2—are the sheep property of Little Bo-Peep? 3—does she have the right to dispose of the sheep? 4—have the sheep been lost, stolen or sold? 5—does Little Bo-Peep have any idea what might have happened to the sheep? 6—does Little Bo-Peep care about the sheep? If we start to think outside the box we can come up with lists of issues that we need to address to consider within the context of our concept. We can think of product aspects and how we might reinvent the product based upon other aspects we are considering. Without a lot of effort we can probably generate a list of alternative scenarios that we should consider.

Next with a little bit of effort we can make up solutions that are reasonable to consider. In response to the question of whether she lost the sheep (third question of the previous paragraph), we might consider what may have happened to the sheep if Little Bo-Peep has the right to dispose of the sheep. For example: 1—can Little Bo-Peep sell the sheep? 2—have the sheep been sold? 3—would Little Bo-Peep sell the sheep or does she want them back? 4—what could cause her to dispose of the sheep? Again thinking outside the box we can come up with a number of possible scenarios.

Below I have provided two variations of the story updated with different scenarios of what the poem might really look like under a different set of assumptions. I have reinvented the story of Little Bo-Peep for you. As a practical matter you should consider reinventing Little Bo-Peep just to see how your new poem would come out.

Our first reinvented nursery rhyme might end up something like this:

A mean old witch has rustled some sheep,
And she will sell them at auction;
The owner will miss them, but the witch will be rich,
As they come home as mutton.

Our second reinvented nursery rhyme might read like the following:

Little Bo-Peep fell asleep,
And her sheep wandered off;
Because they get hungry, they will come home,
Running as fast as they can.

Taking the basic nursery rhyme as our basic concept we can develop an entire set of products for a new set of fractured fairy tales. However, some of these new ideas are not very practical. For example, if we want to continue with the idea of the nursery rhyme as something read to a small child and we are not trying to ruin their life, the first reinvented tale is clearly inappropriate. We do not want the children to think that the sheep have been stolen and killed. In this case the second poem is the preferred product embodiment.

If on the other hand you were born and raised on a cattle ranch, you hate sheep as they destroy the grass where the cattle range. So it might be perfectly acceptable to tell your children about the slaughter of the sheep by the mean old witch.

If we continue to reinvent Little Bo-Peep we might come up with something like this:

Lady Gaga bought some seeds,
And went to plant a garden;
The New York Mayor said no, So she left town,
Planting on Long Island.

Streisand and Kid Rock sang with others,
And really made some hits;
As they sing duets, they'll become standards,
Changing the music scene.

Remember that reinvention is context dependent and what our result will be is determined by the product aspects that we attempt to exploit and the direction that such aspects take us.

We have just shown a number of ways to reinvent the basic ditty of Little Bo-Peep and come up with a number of new versions of ditties that illustrate reinvention.

The key to this positioning is to ask the persistent question of what if and then dive deeper into our alternatives.

CHAPTER 18

Question of "Who Cares?"

One of the problems with trying to reinvent a product and create a disruption was illustrated in Chapter 16. Taking a simple ditty about Little Bo-Peep, I was able to illustrate ways that we could modify the ditty by asking questions and generating a wide range of similar ditties. One thing we need as we go on our journey is the ability to limit the choices we make; otherwise, we will have created a problem bigger than the issue of trying to crawl over pebbles. Our solutions will swamp us.

To accomplish this we will use another comedy routine. In this case we use the Chinese Waiter routine done by Buddy Hackett in the early 60s.In today's society this routine might be considered highly politically incorrect, but it really illustrates the problem of who cares and how we can use that concept to limit our choices. It further illustrates several key issues including: talking over, lack of decision making and how the length of the decision process can derail the design process. You can find a version of the Chinese Waiter on youtube.com at **http://tinyurl.com/749vj4q**.

The basic idea is that 6 people are coming into a Chinese restaurant for dinner. They are looking to get the family dinner. The family dinner is a fixed course dinner where you make a set of selections off of the menu but at times the choices are limited. This process is similar to the design process where we are trying to set the design in the sense of deciding on features that position our product so that someone cares about the product. The similarities between the family trying to get dinner and make decisions are very much like a group of designers trying to design a product. In both cases there will be competing issues throughout the process. The purpose of the Chinese waiter concept is to limit our design issues so that we can make rational solid design. The Chinese Waiter essentially limits the choices available and these choices are further limited by categories because the categories are limited. The purpose of the categories is to provide design structure by cataloging the design choices into categories that we can consider and trade off to articulate our choices.

In the Chinese restaurant the product is well defined. You get a soup, an appetizer, three main dishes and a dessert. Essentially the product choice is simple because you must follow the very simple menu: Soup, appetizer, 3 main dishes and a dessert. This is a well-structured product set. The customer knows what they are getting and has some choice in customizing their specific product. Further, the designers in this case operate much like the designers in a product development but the waiter keeps them on track.

In the initial discussion you have a choice of soup: wonton, egg drop and tomato. There are several problems with this situation. First, there are too many soups ordered (7 for 6 dinners) and then there are too few soups ordered (5). Eventually, the waiter must get this sorted out but before he can make that happen, someone wants split pea soup. There is no split pea soup because it is not on the menu. This is a common problem in that many times the design is moving along and someone wants to order something that we have not previously discussed. They want split pea soup. It is important that we not derail the design process. We cannot at this point allow split pea soup. If we get through a complete design then we can then reexamine the choices and possibilities. But we need to stay focused; through diligent work and cajoling the waiter finally gets the order for the soup—6 soups from the menu of wonton, egg drop or tomato.

This is the same process that you must go through to get your design started correctly. You need to get your people on board and get them focused on going forward using what ifs from the previous step. The soup choice is the start of our design. It is our first modification of the basic concept. If there are issues that we do not understand or need further consideration we should put them on a list for further consideration. But we need to ensure that we move the design forward even if we have to reexamine some decisions at a later date.

The next step, our appetizer, also illustrates a key tradeoff. In the Chinese Waiter sketch we are allowed the choice of spare rib or egg roll not both. We need to make a second choice at this point. It is an easy choice as we need to make a simple selection and it should be easier than our first because now we are used to making decisions and listing alternatives for further consideration. The waiter illustrates the point. He allows us to add both items for an extra cost. In this case it is a cost of 75 cents extra for a second appetizer. This is a key issue. Sometime in the design we may decide to include options and there is a cost for that decision. We do not know what such costs are or will be but every time we make such a decision, we need to document not only the option but its costs and what alternatives might be available.

When designing I like to limit decisions at each level to no more than five or six decisions, with a few of them being key. I want to get started in a simple fashion similar to starting with the soup and appetizer. However, generally, in a product concept you cannot handle six or seven new concepts so really we need to focus on the soup and appetizer. We really need to start with the key decisions. The Chinese Waiter enumerates the main dish decisions as two choices from column a and one choice from column b. Someone invariably tries to change the order or relevance of the decisions. So we need to be careful to avoid taking too many decisions from the second design column. We do not want to select two from column b.

The key is to focus on the biggest design issue we will face and how the product differentiates itself from other products. This is where we pick two or three key concepts that we want to anchor our product around. We need to get focused on the decisions that allow us to differentiate and make our product the definitive product in our design space.

Lastly, we need to put some sizzle into the product. This equates to setting up dessert or sizzle. In the skit, you have the choice of an almond cookie or fortune cookie—no stuffed kumquat. Even though someone may want a stuffed kumquat, they cannot have one if it is not available. It is important that we inject something sweet, provide sizzle or put in a feature or two that will get a serious amount of attention from prospective customers. This area is very difficult and subjective. What grabs one person's attention is very difficult to ascertain in advance. No matter what you try to do, someone will have a serious number of design problems at this point. We're trying to distinguish ourselves from the other potential competitors and it is difficult to really figure out what will create enough sizzle. If we have limited choices, we need to figure out the key issue that will generate a "wow" factor. Remember our choices are fortune cookies and almond cookies—a stuffed kumquat is not available. But, for some reason we are in the restaurant buying dinner. Somehow the restaurant has provided us with the wow factor and we are ordering dinner even though a stuffed kumquat is not possible.

Now comes the last part of the routine. After taking minutes to get the order correct, it took too long to order so "kitchen is closed." This is the part of the routine so common in product development. You are trying to define a product, but you are constantly interrupted or fighting pebbles. when you finally get the product in some state of definition that allows you to go forward, time has run out because someone else has developed or introduced a similar (and potentially equal or better) product. Too many times people have a great idea and for whatever reason are unable to act in a timely fashion. Similarly, many times a person or group who have a prime— (or first—) mover advantage lose out to an aggressive group that may be starting the product race from behind. So they get caught and eclipsed by the aggressive company. It is important to define and act! Conversely, because you do not have the prime-mover advantage does not mean that you will not succeed. Many companies miss the timing on product development and still succeed. Sometimes you can also miss the transition from one product set to another and still survive.

Today the standard seems that a lot of Chinese restaurants have either a buffet or a fixed menu. In times past many Chinese restaurants would have a fixed menu with choices. We want to deal with this aspect of the menu. What makes the routine so appropriate to product development is the idea of limiting choices. In this case the diners must make a choice from a soup and salad and this menu is really fixed to several choices. Then they must make two choices from column a and one choice from column b; they end the order with dessert. This is really the same process we use to set up our design choices.

This simple process allows us to get our product to the "who cares" question. If one customer wants to order split pea soup, which is not on the menu, the issue has to be resolved. Clearly if the customer is insistent on split pea soup, this is not the restaurant for him. There is also the problem of the number of soups and salads to order. This is like weeding out the basic required features that we want in our product.

Then we come to the main part, our "entrees." In this case we need to pick two items from column a and one from column b. This is like trying to pick a couple of features that will excite our customer base and cause them to purchase our product. Further, once we have our categories we need a couple of detailed examples of capabilities or benefits that we are going to include in the product.

Lastly, we pick our dessert and thus the sizzle we intend to use for our product. At this point we have defined our dinner. This is a unique dinner but at the table we may have up to six uniquely defined dinners. Each dinner corresponds to a product definition (component, product or system) that provides us with a cohesively packaged set of definitions of a product that helps us as we try to estimate the potential customer base. Just because we have a product defined there is no reason to assume that someone will actually buy the product. At this point we want to take each complete concept and determine the potential customers and the size of the market. Only then do we have any idea if this product is attractive enough to be sold and whether it has the differentiation necessary to create a disruption.

Innovate then refine. We are not through with the product definition. We probably will not have a well-defined product at this point. What we've done is take a set of "what ifs" and tried to develop and position our product. We will have inconsistencies. There are areas that are open to interpretation. We might be tempted to revisit the product definition at this point, but I want to keep going. Here is the problem. If we stop now and revisit or try to tune up our product we will get into issues that I feel (from experience) are really secondary issues. We will get bogged down in arguments over details that are not really relevant at this point. I want to go to the next step before we revisit any part of the process.

The key to the restaurant business—a few key entrees and no bad food! Also, no food poisoning! The key to the product definition business—a few key new features!

Now having defined the product we can finally answer the question of how the potential customer base feels about our product.

CHAPTER 19

Question of
"Market Size?"

For our product to be successful it must have a market. In the previous step, we tried to build a complete product specification. We may have built several different product concepts—our work load may have increased. Now we need to take each product idea and figure out where the product fits from a customer perspective. Once we have determined where the product fits, we can then estimate the size of the market.

We are now at the place where the rubber meets the road. If we cannot find a potential set of customers for each product idea we have generated, the game is over. We must identify a customer and only then can we build an estimate of possible market size.

How we grab the attention of a customer is a difficult question. We briefly discussed the concept of wow, but we need something that really grabs our potential customer base. In this vein (if we are trying to create a disruption) we need to believe that our potential customer base will latch onto our product. If we can get a customer base that is inspired we can then build our estimates.

We are now far beyond wow!

We want the customer's attention. We want the customer demanding our product. We need the customer to talk to all of their friends about how great our product is. We want to generate buzz and demand. How we get there is not easily accomplished due to the large amount of information and number of products in the marketplace at any given time!

I want a product that will meet what I call the John Denver criteria. John was a 70s folk singer of note. At his concerts he would shout "Far Out" at various points. If we are to create a truly disruptive technology we need to get that same reaction from our customers. Looking at the product definition we need to determine what type of customer will react to our far out shout. If we can energize the customer base, we can get them to forget the potential competitive products and view us as the "must have" disruptive product—a product that they will brag to their friends about because it is so cool everyone should own one.

One of the problems we face at this point is that we have reinvented this product. We are biased to the idea that this is a product with the potential to disrupt the marketplace and we need to step back and take a critical look at the reality of our product.

It may seem strange but the first issue we must address is reality. What is it? We take a careful and critical look at the product, trying to estimate what the potential customer will really think about the product. Can we even describe potential customers and their characteristics? Do we really know what will excite them and make them buy our product? What do we need to do to reliably figure out how to sell our product?

As an example, ask yourself whether you have ever encountered a new born baby that a gathering of people would describe as being ugly. Every time I have been around a group of people talking about someone's newborn baby, the talk always turns to how cute the baby is. Under this scenario there are no ugly babies. Yet, there must be some ugly babies.

There also must be product concepts that are just terrible. In fact, they may be so bad that they are ridiculous. Yet every product has a designer who believes that the product is worth something and people should buy it. If we cannot get an accurate estimate of the product's pull on potential customers, we will never be able to estimate its value.

This is where "far out" comes into play. If we are to grab the attention of the customer, we must be able to describe our product in a way that excites the customer. Further, we must energize the press. If we can energize the press we will get the customer's attention. Because of the vast mass of new products being developed we must be able to describe our product in terms of value that the customer will want. If we are trying to develop a truly disruptive product we must, at this point, describe the product in a fashion that really wakes up the community. The way to do this is to take the product descriptions that we have developed and recast them (starting with our twenty-five word description) in terms that identify and highlight the "far out" aspects of the product.

When this is accomplished we are still not ready to try to build our market estimates. We need to reach people in the press and explain what is unique, what the grabber is and how far out our product really is. We need to set our product apart.

Given the reaction of the press we can then refine our product descriptions and move forward.

Why do I want to go to the press? Well it is really quite simple. The press sees a lot of products. They see almost every new product that is brought onto the market and they tend to know what is selling because successful companies court the press. We are trying to tap into that knowledge base.

We need to find who is writing about our area in the trade press and then court that person so they will look at our product. Checking the bloggers under the more tab in Google is one place to start this process. If after looking at our product they do not seem interested or they explain how our product is similar to some other product we are back to the drawing board. It is when they tell us our product seems pretty cool and they would like to write about it that we are in the home stretch. Unfortunately at this point we only have a concept, but we can make an estimate as to when we will have the product available. And, we can offer them an exclusive look at the product and tell them when they will get their scoop. We need to keep them in the loop as we develop the product so that we continue to get feedback as the product develops.

Now we move onto the market size issue. When we have passed through the model to the point at which we now have a product and a description that is "far out," we need to estimate our product's market potential.

Since we have reinvented something (or used variations on several products) we can begin the process by discovering the size of the market for the product(s) we used as the basis of the reinvention. Once we have these basic market sizes there are a number of questions that must be answered.

First, is it our intent to dislodge and try to kill another product? Or, are we thinking that we will be creating a variation on the original products and our product will not destroy portions of the market but expand the overall market? Thus, we can begin to build a market size estimate. It is important to determine whether there are a couple of extant products that comprise the market and whether our product can potentially kill these products by selling a higher function at a lower cost. If so we are in trouble because we may be destroying the market while providing no way for us to really capitalize on our efforts. An example of such a market is the airline industry. Every airline tries to kill the others but the only value is cost and so periodically the airlines run out of money and they go bankrupt because there is no product differentiation.

Second, the easiest way to accomplish our goal is to seek a market concept that will cause the market to expand. It is even better if we injure competitive products when we introduce our product. The combination of destroying the competition while simultaneously opening a new market is the key to a successful launch of a new product. We want and need buzz, rapid product acceptance and a shortage of product to make the demand for our product soar. Measuring and estimating such effects are going to be difficult but not impossible as we will divide up the estimation into a series of well-defined steps.

Third, product overlap is a key starting point for our market analysis. Looking at customer aspects associated with our product we know about a number of different customer types. We need to look at each possible customer type and determine what, if any, products in the market are similar to our product. Because each product that is similar has a market and sales, we can determine what the sales are, what type of customer is buying the product and how the existing product relates to our product. Specifically, we wish to determine any overlaps to the position or capabilities of our product. It is from this customer analysis and product analysis that we will be able to estimate what sales we can steal due to the positioning of our product and the size of the customer base for the variations or feature sets of our products. The goal here is to generate a series of estimates for sales contributions from different variations of our products across the customer base. Different revenue streams are the simplest way to look at product overlap. Consider that we own an entertainment venue and have a sports team. Some customers simply buy the basic product, a ticket. They sneak their peanuts into the venue. Other customers buy parking and concessions as well as their ticket. Other customers buy memorabilia. Some upper income customers buy luxury suites to entertain customers. They also buy expensive and elaborate food and beverage service. In a city there may be multiple teams playing at the same time of the year so we must determine how events overlap and how to capture as many entertainment dollars as possible. We are in competition with the other teams for coverage in news outlets such as newspaper sports pages and radio and television. We're trying to obtain the largest network of radio and television stations to handle our broadcasts. Further, we want the stations with large audiences. We also are in competition to obtain sponsors and personal deals for our athletes. There are also revenues associated with our programs and other events we can develop. The strategy is to break up each way of generating revenue and each segment of revenue. We can then compare them to other similar products and we can get an estimate of what we can realistically expect in terms of revenue.

Fourth, market capture analysis is our next step. What we mean here is that given our new product, we should have (due to the nature of reinvention and our attempt to create disruption) uniqueness associated with our product. We need an estimate of what we can expect from the exploitation of such product proper-ties. At this point we are going to have to develop "blue sky" estimates. If we have done our job correctly we have put in place capabilities that make our product attractive with a strategy that can take our early sales with small groups to sales dominated by large mass consumer characteristics. At this point we do not have any product overlap to rely upon for our estimates. We will have to find information that illustrates how products in similar industries were able to grow over time. This is complicated—we may not find product data or industry data that is directly comparable in time frame or potential market size. Thus, we are really making large and complicated guesses at this point. One of the keys is to docu-ment all assumptions so when we get better data or more knowledge we can update our analysis. One of the most used strategies is to take a percentage of the market to determine how much of that market we can capture. One percent is not an acceptable estimate. Everybody says "if I can just capture one percent . . ." once you have said that everyone know that you do not know what you are talking about. It is easy to postulate a giant market and then say you only need one percent. Do your homework and build a real-istic model.

Fifth, new market engagement tactics are keys to our anal-ysis. If you really want to capture the revenues streams that you talk about, how do you plan to accomplish that? Usual analysis is to rely upon the size of the market. I am expecting more. I want overlap analysis and uniqueness analysis, but I also want to know how you intend to gain the market share that you are projecting. Is it through distributors? Do you plan to put a coffee shop on each corner of every sixth block in every major metropolitan area? Just how can you specify your market penetration strategy so that I will believe that you stand a chance to meet your estimates? This step is critical because analysis helps us understand how we may have to change our strategy based upon competitive reaction. Did we think about possible competitive reactions? What will we do if our initial strategy does not work? How can we go about evolving our strategies and how do we know what is working? There are a lot of questions that we need to answer so that we can feel confident in our analysis. We do not just want to postulate a scenario and hope that everything works out for the best. We need to actively plan for problems. We need alternatives that we could consider if we need to make some changes to our basic strategy.

Sixth, estimation of the market will be our next step. Many people try to estimate the market and they give you a specific number or percentage of the market that they will capture. I want to approach the problem differently. We have previously developed the basic information that we need and I just want to extend it. What I am looking for is a market analysis that brackets the potential market opportunity by detailing the sources of revenue that I believe that I can obtain by selling to a portion of the market and the technique that I can use to obtain that market position. I want to know how and why I get my revenue streams. I also want to know what the bounds on each type of revenue are and what probability I have of achieving that revenue goal. I do not want to simply add up the individual revenue components and say that is the answer. I want to know about interactions between components of revenue and how they can be related. Does the fact that I can increase one portion of revenue mean that I am cannibalizing part of another revenue source? This type of analysis may seem overkill, but if I am trying to introduce and market a disruptive product I need to think about lots of possible consequences. Note that I did not say *all* of the consequences because if my product is truly disruptive I do not know what will happen when it is unleashed on the world so I need to do a lot of thinking about alternatives.

Seventh, growth estimates now become important. My estimates and the estimates of the relative revenue components are now key issues. The fundamental issue that I am faced with is dynamic analysis. Once I begin to go down the track I will be faced with the problem of a changing world. I need to try to account for that in my estimates and to do this I must begin to think about how the estimates will change in time. I need to think about how to project this information into the future and what possible interactions are possible.

Eighth, comparison analysis now becomes important as we need to figure out whether our product compares favorably with the products of others. Unless we provide a compelling value we run the risk of two serious problems. One is that our product does not compare well against other alternatives. In this case we have the problem that we will have difficulty getting the attention of the consumer and we will not be able to get to the volumes that we desire. The other issue to worry about is that if we conceived of a complex product that is too far out then it could be difficult to make the consumer understand the value of our product against alternatives. It is not just good enough to have a quality product but we must also make sure it is well positioned and easily understood from a value and capability perspective.

Ninth, worst-case scenarios now come into play. After we have gone through our complete analysis we need to develop a set of scenarios that describe our possible total outcomes. In most cases we're in position and we think we're on the right track. But what if we are on the wrong track and the product we are developing or its sales start to go in the wrong direction? What if nobody cares? What if the product definition is off? What if there is just no market? We need to begin planning for events that are not pleasant and what we can do to recover or change our approach. This last step is critical as we are trying to develop a real product and we do not know where we will end up. What if, for example, demand goes way beyond what we allowed for and we have unsatisfied customers due to our inability to deliver product in a timely fashion. Even worse what if we are doing a one-of-a-kind product and our estimates are completely out of line. If they were too high and the customer finds out that we are making a fortune they could view us as profiteers. A worse case is that the estimate was too low and we cannot deliver the product at all.

Chapter 20
Use of Model

In the preceding chapters and sections we have discussed the issues of developing a product and ways to go about the process. We need to stay focused and concentrate on the matter at hand. We need to move forward, content with the knowledge that no product is perfect. That being said I have found that humor is a good way to keep us on track and focused on the big picture. Although we have discussed many of the issues in detail, I present a short summary below so that we remember where we have come and where we are heading.

Create: Define a concept (Pick a card—any card) and describe the concept succinctly (Twenty-five words or less)

Reinvent: Develop what ifs (Little Bo-Peep)

Position: Define product/concept variations (Chinese Waiter)

Disrupt: Define customer base and size markets (Far out)

Repeat: (iterate the above steps)

Part III Conclusion

We have just gone through the fundamentals of using our model. We have used humor to illustrate ways to force the process forward. We reemphasize the need for focus and not letting pebbles get in our way of the product definition. Lack of precision is important as we need some flexibility to ensure that we have developed a good product. A very precise product will never be possible as no product is perfect. That being said in part 4 we will provide some examples of successful and unsuccessful products and how they evolved or were reinvented.

We are trying to use a disciplined approach to the problem at hand. Products do not just jump out of the sky. They are the result of hard work and enterprise over a period of time. The old routine of Johnny Carson, Carnac the Magnificent, where he divines the question given the answer does not work in product development.

We are trying to systematically develop a product concept that we can sell and get consumers to want. Think of this in regards to owning a baseball team (or other sports team) and what we have to do to get consumer interest. Another way to think about the problem is to think about the process of buying a car. What is going to excite the buyer? In the 70s and 80s it was fuel economy and reliability. The fact that some companies completely missed these issues and had high labor costs led to the demise of major American auto manufacturers until they were bailed out by the government.

Lastly, consider that in many cases your product will be scored (selected) on the basis of a check list built and used by the consumer. In boxing's 10-point rule (or must system) which is used in Nevada you get ten points for each round (factor) on which you beat your competitor. Yet, you can win the business or fight by knocking out the competition. At which point the score no longer matters. Creative disruption attempts to be so disruptive of the status quo that we will get a knock out on each product that we attempt to build. Our goal is not to get the most points. It's the knockout that wins the business!

PART IV

EXAMPLES OF PRODUCT STRATEGIES

In this part we will examine case studies of products. We will examine some products that were only conceived, some that were prototyped and some that made it to high volume production. Some discussions I find amusing. Some I find only interesting. But, all will be illustrative of the basic ideas of reinvention previously presented in this book.

The examples come from a variety of categories including automotive, computer, music, art, consumer and industry. The variety provides a set of case studies that illustrate various factors of reinvention ranging from successful to fanciful failures.

CHAPTER 21

Example of Executive PC

In the early days of the personal computer (PC) revolution, there were a number of people struggling to figure out the value and worth of the PC. When Apple introduced its products many people thought of them as toys or hobby computers. Eventually, even though the products had limited capabilities, people began to think of them as serious pieces of equipment.

Then, IBM brought out the IBM PC and the game changed. People began to think of the PC as something that might be useful in a business. The IBM brand gave the PC legitimacy.

It is in this context that I first met the "Executive PC."

Let's think a little about history. At first people did not really know what to think of personal computers. In fact, if you had one you were the local gadget guy and people were in awe. Today they are ubiquitous and everyone has one including the one in your phone. But humor me and let's go back in time.

Everyone was focusing on the IBM PC as the new business paradigm.

In the confusion surrounding a new emerging technology there were issues of how to use the PC. What kind of person should and could use such a device? In many cases the early users were clerical staff using it as an alternative to a typewriter. Some programmers used it as a smart terminal and business analysts liked it for its spreadsheet capabilities.

A big issue then was what could you use the PC for in business. You know the question, what if?

There were all kinds of scenarios but one hot topic of debate was how the PC fit into the executive suite because at that time many executives did not know how to type.

One day I was sitting innocently in my office when my phone rang and a buddy who was in the investment business rang me up to chat. He had a big scoop. The next day there was going to be a big article in the press about the Executive PC that had been developed by a local company and he had arranged an appointment for us to get a preview because he was thinking of investing in the company. He assured me that the Executive PC was awesome.

A meeting was set and soon I was on my way to meet him to get the pitch. It was a great pitch. Their facilities were first class. They had a professional presentation and knew what they were talking about. The issues of the day were succinctly presented. They went over all of the key user issues about the PC and its potential for revolutionizing the office automation market. They talked about the barriers the PC would encounter in the executive suite and kept us in suspense about their solution.

Finally, they dealt with the big issue. The need for and impediments the PC would face in the executive suite. But they claimed that they would soon show us their breakthrough device that would put the PC firmly in the hands of executives. Not only that but their device was not vaporware (a product that is announced but never released) because they had one operating and it was in the office of their founder and CEO. It was being used by him and it was really a revolutionary device. For the rest of the presentation we would go to his office and be able to see the Executive PC in action.

We went to the CEO's office and beheld the great device.

The Executive PC was a repackaged PC. The designers

thought the real impediment to ubiquitous use and deployment of PC technology was that it came in a crummy looking metal case and that executives would not want such a terrible looking piece of equipment sitting on their desk. So they asked the question, what if we repackaged the PC by replacing its case (and building a case that would fit around the monitor) so that the Executive PC would fit into the executive's furniture scheme. There was no change or addition in function to the PC, just versions that came in oak, walnut or cherry. The Executive PC was a simple PC with a wood enclosure that could be selected to match the executive's furniture! And, it was gorgeous.

They had done a great job of asking the question, what if? But had forgotten to ask the question of who cares. The real value of reinventing the PC wasn't making it look pretty but in its utility.

My friend, the investor, was not known for his technical savvy but even he realized the absurdity of the situation. We politely listened to the rest of the pitch and went on our way. The next day the Executive PC became the laughing stock of our office as people read about it and had very negative comments about the designers and their lack of insight about the emerging business.

The designers were on the right track. What if? And, they had a solution. There was just one problem. No one cared about their solution!

There could have been other ways to approach this problem. What if you improved the functions (software application developers profited from this strategy)? What if you made the PC easier to use (graphical interface users like Apple and Microsoft made money with variations of this strategy)? What if you built functions that could be built into boards that plugged into the slots in the PC so users could customize their product? And, if I wanted to, I could give you a long list of variations that would have made you money. However, the idea of repackaging the PC into a classy wood case was not any idea that would let you make money under any circumstances! Another choice with a higher probability of success would have been to harden it for industrial and military applications. Just because you can define a "what if" scenario does not mean that anyone cares or that there is a market. Reinvention needs a context and customer base to have any chance of success.

LESSON

The PC market promise was not one of form. It was a promise of massive productivity improvements and a potential shift in the way business was done. Concentrating on irrelevancies rather than on results will doom your business to obscurity.

CHAPTER 22

Example of Laser Computer

In the late 60s and early 70s there was a trend in the computer industry to try and build large scale systems with different capabilities. One area was laser memories. Another area was large scale computers. In the computer business sometimes it is difficult to separate fact from fiction. And, in fact, fiction may be very believable.

One of the big issues at the time was large memories. Another was high speed computer systems, particularly real time computer systems for a variety of tasks. At the time there were a large number of people participating in the marketplace with a variety of approaches. In fact, many of the market participants would today be considered unorthodox including many members of the aerospace and defense industry. There were also a large number of ideas being bandied about including non-volatile memory for many applications, radiation-hardened systems for military and satellite systems and high-performance systems for intelligence applications.

But, one of the most interesting systems was announced by Frank Marchuk. In terms of the "what if" question, Frank Marchuk announced a Laser Computer. The what if in this case is pretty simple. What if he really had developed and could produce a computer with the properties that were described? Then, the answer to the second question is pretty simple. Who cares? Every intelligence agency and military computer user in the world cares.

A laser computer is an interesting concept. At the time there was talk of building laser based memory systems. If you can build a memory and then build some logic around it you could build a computer. If you could build the logic using some type of laser logic it would be even better, but we digress.

If we could build a laser computer then you would obtain higher density of memory storage and potentially higher computation speeds than anything in existence at the time. This would be attractive to lots of users. The benefits of such a computer would restructure the entire industry. So there was a lot of interest in the product.

The Marchuk Laser Computer answered two questions: what if? And who cares? However, the product was not real. "What if?" postulated an answer that would blow the doors off all product reinvention aspects. It had technology, features, benefits, value-add and new system capabilities as aspects to make a case for it as a transforming product. It answered the "who cares?" question with a number of well-heeled big buck potential customers ranging from intelligence agencies to businesses like banks, all of whom could use such a system. It could have put IBM out of business. If it had gone further it would have smashed the question of market size because everyone was clamoring to get their hands on the laser computer.

But, it had one potential fatal flaw. It did not exist and does not exist today. But, how do we know it does not exist? We don't. But, if it exists, it is one of the best kept secrets in the known world on par with the alien autopsy in Roswell New Mexico.

And, even better, if it exists, then the large government users (intelligence agencies, military and civilian agencies such as social security) of such computers are buying billions of dollars of commercial-off-the-shelf equipment each year to keep the secret a secret and keeping employment high by buying such inferior products.

This is a classic case study of technology advancement dreams being unrealistic. We are talking about optical memory forms, laser computers and finally the coupé de grace, the atomic computer. Having not found its way into Ripley's Believe It or Not, I include some references for your perusal. There is, however, some amount of literature surrounding the laser computer and some pointers to articles about this interesting idea are provided:

http://tinyurl.com/7jnrvrz—optical memory

http://tinyurl.com/7mafuqu—laser computer

http://tinyurl.com/6t279dm—laser computer

http://tinyurl.com/7f76kps—atomic computer

The idea of the laser computer is spectacular. It fulfills all the necessary aspects of reinvention. The what if of the idea gets us to who cares (a lot of powerful and rich customers) which gets us a large potential market size (everyone wants one). But the problem is that the what if was not (at least at that time) possible. Although it's not close to being practical, it is desired by large groups and it is a potentially transforming technology. It just did not happen.

A November 2011 article in the CACM (Communications of the Association of Computing Machinery) discusses nanocomputers, computers built using nanotechnology and nanonetworks, so maybe Marchuk was just forty or fifty years ahead of his time. However, the article clearly articulates the alternatives and technical challenges that must be overcome to create such computers. No time frame is given but the article makes it

LESSON

No matter how great an idea is, it must be supported by reality. You cannot generate a product (profit) if you are detached from the technical realities of the possible.

seem that the ideas are eventually possible. With the emphasis on such technologies maybe the future does contain nanocomputers and nanonetworks. In this case the stumbling block remains being able to realize a solution to what if.

CHAPTER 23

Example of Pony Cars

One of the great success stories in the automobile business is "pony cars." The name really derives from the Ford Mustang, first introduced in the 60s. Ford Mustang was so successful that it spawned a complete category of automobiles that has lasted till today—known as the pony car category after the Mustang.

Let's review how this product was born. In the early 60s Ford was producing a terrible little car, the Ford Falcon. This was an econobox was terrible to drive and had a horrible ride. As it got to the end of its product cycle (based upon sales volume and technology), Ford decided to discontinue the product. Yet the car had a basic chassis and engine combination and Ford made the decision to bring out a new vehicle based on this platform. This vehicle would be known as the Ford Mustang.

The original Ford Mustang was really just a reinvention of the Falcon. Ford slapped bucket seats, a floor shift and some interior cosmetic improvements into a new set of sheet metal and the Mustang was born. The basic question, What If?, was answered by just modifying the platform and developing a new product. The question, Who Cares?, was quickly answered as the Mustang sold quickly and made lots of headlines. The answer to the question of

Market Size? One word-Big!

This is an example of a very successful product concept and launch that propelled the new vehicle into a high volume position and instant success. At this point the Thunderbird, Ford's previous "sports car," had morphed into a four seater and had essentially failed as a product ceding the space to the Chevrolet Corvette. But, the Mustang with its lower price point and good looks looked like it could turn this situation around. The Mustang had the added advantage because it did not compete directly with the Corvette in either price or performance.

Ford had done a great job of asking the right questions, understanding the answers and positioning the product. But from a performance standpoint it was a slug compared to the sports cars of the day. As soon as they heard that type of comment, Ford began reinventing its own product. If someone is going to obsolete your product it had better be you because you do not want to allow the competition to obsolete your product or get a jump on your market. This is particularly true when you invent the category.

Reinvention of the Mustang was a simple problem. Give it a bigger engine. Give it better suspension. Change the transmission. Generally, beef up the car in ways that allow it to meet customer expectations. And these expectations were defined by the look of the vehicle. Because of the look, people expected the car to have a certain feel and capability, particularly a powerful engine in terms of horsepower and torque.

Over time the Mustang has had numerous variations and reinventions. There have been smaller more economical versions like the Mustang II. This was a throwback vehicle that was not really true to the virtues of the Mustang. It tried to dominate the pony car segment of the market with the slogan "Mustang two, boredom zero." In fact as a pony car or small muscle car the Mustang II was a boring loser.

Ford has had the most success with the Mustang when it has kept it beefed up and not boring. When its reinventors lapse into considerations of economy and gas mileage, then the car drifts into a bad image and sales posture. When the car has very high performance versions available and has that racing image it is quite successful. It is the image or sizzle that keeps the buyers coming in the door.

Chevrolet has not been as successful at this as Ford. They introduced the Camero which at times has beaten up on the Mustang, but at times they have discontinued or deemphasized the vehicle. The Camero is the car to judge the Mustang against and the Mustang holds up very well over an extended time frame.

The real key to the Mustang's success was that it was positioned away from both the Thunderbird and Corvette so it kept its position as the long standing pony car that defined a genre. Even though it has had its problems completely dominating the market during its continuing reinvention process, it has been a money maker for Ford.

As an example of successful reinvention you would do well to follow the success of the Mustang. The vehicle has gone through lots of reinvention and it has had its sour moments in different eras, but it has always stayed successful and made money.

The original projections were that the Mustang (introduced in April 1964) would sell 100,000 units in its first year. It sold over 1,000,000 in its first 18 months with about 480,000 of those in the first year. The day after its introduction it was written up in nearly 2,600 newspapers. Using a reinvention strategy provided a clear winner for a new car. Over the years the Mustang has become larger and more muscular at the top of its line and still retains its every day driver formula. The Mustang is the only pony car to have remained in production for over four decades. There are now five generations of Mustangs with model variations within each generation. The Mustang is a very successful example of reinvention.

The automobile business is an example of a target rich environment for reinvention. Look at all the specialty cars that have been developed. Take muscle cars , for example, as illustrated by the genre-creating Pontiac GTO. Consider the emerging hybrid and electric car market. Additionally, there are all types of specialty parts manufacturers of everything from wheels and tires to engine and body parts. Lastly, there are numerous manufacturers or modifiers of cars like "tuners," people who develop and sell limited production specialty cars such as the GT-40 and Shelby Cobra. Car modification has become such a large business that even manufacturers such as Ford have divisions engaged in such business, like Ford's SVT (Special Vehicle Team). Reinventing the automobile is a fertile long term business opportunity.

LESSON

Continual reinvention will allow a sustainable product set over an extended period of years. Success requires that you capture the hearts and minds of the consumer. You can never let up because the competition is always after you. The return of the Camaro is based in part on the computer graphics of a popular movie—Transformers. This has made Ford react and step up its game.

CHAPTER 24
Example of Starbucks

Starbucks is a great example of reinvention over and over and over again. In this case, we start with a group of people who are roasting coffee beans and happy doing it. The corporation reinvents itself where it has stores everywhere (well nearly) and sells not only roasted beans but also specialty drinks as well as sandwiches and salads. In the beginning, they had a specialty: taking raw beans, roasting them and then putting them in packages. In particular, the roasters tried to avoid selling the beans as finished product. But this is Seattle and it is on the way to becoming the coffee counter-culture capital of the world, so the roasters soon found themselves in a dilemma. Should they just keep roasting or should they move into other avenues of coffee sales? The start of the reinvention was providing sample drinks of coffee at the site of the roasting. But what got the ball rolling was the merger (takeover/purchase) of the roaster by a retail coffee shop. It is at this point that the name changes from Starbuck to Starbucks and the die is cast.

As the coffee business heats up, Starbucks steps out and starts putting up a lot of coffee shops in Seattle and surrounding environs. Then it begins to branch out. They develop and add products. They acquire. They put in food. They try different branding—

even distribution of popular new CD releases.

All of the above activities are anchored around having the basic coffee business (selling beans and drinks) located in as many places as possible. In the early days they stuck to selling beans and giving away a few free sample drinks, but acquisition of the basic business by Il Giornale (a coffee shop business owned by a former executive of Starbucks) and the rebranding of Il Giornale to Starbucks started a rapid expansion push.

In detail, this is a strategy of brand identity creating easy access to a wide variety of specialty products that makes everyone think of the brand when buying or considering buying a cup of coffee. They open individual stores as fast as possible, they buy up other coffee shops (Seattle's Best, Diedrich and Coffee People), they go into other retail locations (Barnes and Noble and even a cruise ship). They even begin to try branding other restaurants under different names (although they are discovered and have to rename their Circadia restaurants as Starbucks cafes), they add food including salads and a variety of pastries and sandwiches and they start to sell other impulse items such as music.

And, they set up operations all over the world.

But the critical aspects of this push are to create a recognizable brand that is internationally ubiquitous. Part of the strategy is to have branded stores inside other stores. Another part is to develop new products (like specialty music) that can be pushed through existing stores.

Lastly, as they reinvent they become aggressive. Think about the coffee business. It is really pretty simple. You sell a drink that essentially costs nothing in a nice cup with your logo. Next, you can create specialty drinks that take longer to produce but get a higher price. As the customers wait in line they have been queued up and you can present other items to generate an impulse buy: rolls, salads, and sandwiches. So the reinvention is pretty simple. You have your basic coffee product and you keep extending your available items as customers pass through the turnstiles.

Next we need a business strategy. If we can place enough

stores at enough locations, then you have a mass market and can catch customers as they stream by. The key is to get a lot of stores in concentrated markets and build your brand name. I know a neighborhood where there are two Starbucks on the same street two blocks apart and on the same side of the street. I have also encountered stores across the street from each other or stores in a shopping center where just around the corner there's a Barnes and Noble containing a Starbucks. One of the strategies is to make the presence so ubiquitous that the mass consumer is constantly bombarded with your product.

There is however business practice issues that Starbucks is chastised for from consumer groups. They will try to saturate a market and have been known to buy out successful competitors leases. There are concerns about their environmental impact, but they have embraced recycling. They have had labor disputes. And, they have been attacked by the coffee efforts of McDonalds who claim to have the best and cheapest coffee.

Yet they have grown rapidly and successfully.

All of which shows that reinvention is possible in even mundane businesses like coffee. To have a shot at the brass ring, you need to build a ubiquitous and readily identifiable brand and stock the stores that you have located everywhere with simple goods that can be easily and quickly produced. Further, you must be attuned to consumer trends and reinvent your product mix periodically, latching onto consumer trends in fashion and music.

LESSON

For a mundane business, reinvention is critical to survival. Innovation and consumer understanding allow for rapid expansion of new ideas regardless of their complexity.

CHAPTER 25

Example of Segway

We have briefly talked about the Segway in previous parts of this book. I clearly think that transportation modes such as Segway are very useful and interesting tools. There are many situations in large structures and warehouses in which you would like to get around in a hurry but distance prevents that. If, however, you can ride on a simple vehicle the job of movement would be much easier.

You could clearly accomplish this task using several means. You could use a bicycle. You could use a golf cart. Or you could run or have a moving belt. Clearly, these could all be considered as useful devices.

You could also reinvent the means of transportation and develop a product like the Segway. But the question you have to ask is who cares. The Segway has shown that some portion of the market for alternative transportation cares, but not a large segment.

From a technology perspective, the Segway is taking the inverted pendulum algorithm and implementing it in a two wheel vehicle. Normal pendulums pivot from their top point as they are designed to hang in the down position and swing in an arc from the pivot point. An example is a clock pendulum. Inverted pendulums pivot from their bottom point and are inherently an unstable system unless they are stabilized. This stabilization process is akin to keeping a broom upright when you balance it on your finger while holding the broom stick upside down. The inverted pendulum, unless stabilized, will tip over.

Given an inverted pendulum-based vehicle, would that give you a way to create some sort of business? If you did implement the algorithm you could make a self-aware two-wheeled vehicle that makes movement convenient. But even though the product is easy to define, how big is the market?

We all see Segways out driving around. One of their main uses is tours of major cities. They have a lot of uses but they never did fulfill their promise of giant market size. There are a lot of uses. For example, law enforcement can cover large areas such as airports with ease. But the perceived need for a high degree of skill and balance to operate the Segway has been a market killer. High price compared to alternatives such as bicycles also has been a problem. To counter the balance/skill issue, a three wheeler was the solution. There is no solution to the price issue.

If we examine our three questions we can conclude that the Segway is cute but not a big winner in creating a transportation industry disruption.

LESSON

Great ideas must provide a real and tangible benefit available via no other means. It is not good enough to have pizazz if there are other alternative solutions that can change the cost equation.

If we implement the inverted pendulum algorithm, then from a technology perspective we can show a unique product. If we define our base product as the Segway platform that we see being driven around, then we have defined a salable product. We have all the aspects of a successful product, but the market size does not create a ubiquitous product. Thus, the product generates a lot of buzz and some sales but is not disruptive.

Prior to its introduction and sale speculation about the Segway was hyped to extreme levels. People were comparing it to the Internet and PC revolution, but the product has not measured up to its hype. It's a nice interesting product but no game changer.

CHAPTER 26
Example of Las Meninas

Barcelona is a great and interesting city. It is home to a really interesting population with a large number of well-known innovators and reinventors. Consider the artist Picasso. He was born in Malaga and in his early teens his family moved to Barcelona where he worked on his art career at the Barcelona School of Fine Arts. Picasso later studied at the Madrid Royal Academy of San Fernando. He later moved to Paris. For a while, he split his time between Barcelona and Paris. If you go to the Barcelona museum (Museu Picasso), celebrating his work and career, you will see an accomplished artist but also a great reinventor.

Over time he studied art and became a reasonable young artist, but his success would come much later in life when he created a whole new form of art. Let us examine how his career as a reinventor progressed.

Picasso's works evolved through major periods of his career. The first period was his early art and training. During this time, Picasso developed "regular" art. He produced, sold and accepted commissions for portraits, landscapes and this was also the start of his interest in realism or modernism. But he was not satisfied and had difficulty adhering to the standards of the time. Eventually he moved to Paris to be with more avant-garde artists and thus began his "blue" period. In this period, he experimented with paintings that contained a large amount of the color blue. Generally these paintings were of a form that was similar to his first period paintings. They were not too far out, although the color palate was highly restricted. This is important because it showed that he wanted to be more aggressive but his work still had to deal with the remnants of his earlier training. Yet, he was asking the what if question. What if I restrict my color palate and at the same time make the subject matter more unusual. In this case the product was different, similar in concept to that by other avant-garde artists because it was art that was trying to stretch the boundaries of taste and it could be sold to the art clientele who were looking for the latest thing.

His next period was his "rose period." This again featured a restricted palate and he painted in cheery colors with many pictures using circus people and performers. From there he moved into an African period which was inspired and influenced by African artifacts. After that, he moved on to periods of cubism, classicism and surrealism. Later in his career he began to produce reinterpretations of the great masters.

What was important was that Picasso discovered his market for paintings that did not correspond to the norms of contemporary art. This success allowed him to begin developing what has since become known as the cubist art form. In this form Picasso began to make oddly shaped and bright colored abstractions of surreal views of scenes and people. This was an aggressive reinvention of his blue period. This is where he moved further out in both subject matter and the way the art forms were presented—not only how they were presented, but also their color and structure.

But in my opinion his greatest achievement (and one of, if not the best example of reinvention that I have ever seen) was his reinvention of Las Meninas. Las Meninas is a famous painting by the Spanish artist Diego Velazquez. It is a scene of a royal family (King Phillip IV of Spain) sitting in a large room. The painting has several key points. The family has a number of members seated at various points in a room. In his style, Velazquez illustrates the ability to see through the room by strategically placing a window and door. Further, the picture contains an illustration of a dog and child and two maids of honor along with Velazques himself. In a mirror located on the back wall are the reflections of the monarchs Phillip IV and Mariana of Austria. There are other figures in the painting as well. The open door and window, allowing you to see outside, are also significant portions of the painting. This is one of the most famous paintings by a Spanish artist and can be seen in the Prada art museum in Madrid.

Velazquez is considered to be the leading artist of the Spanish Golden Age. Las Meninas is one of the most analyzed paintings and is considered to be very important. This is an important painting that Picasso liked and in his later years decided to reinterpret.

Picasso liked both the painting and the painter's work. However, he decided to redo the painting in his own style. He reinvented Las Meninas. But, for whatever reason, he was not satisfied at his own attempts and continued to reinvent Las Meninas. He reinvented parts of the painting. He reinvented his own interpretation of the entire painting numerous times. In the Picasso Museum in Barcelona, they dedicate an entire gallery to the reinvention of Las Meninas. You can see how Picasso, in painting parts of the painting, reinvented not only the work of Valzquez but his own versions of the painting.

The coup de grace is an exhibit near the end of the gallery. This is the greatest monument to reinvention I have ever seen. At this location there is a sequence of projected video overlays that indicate how portions of the various versions of his paintings overlay parts of the original in concept and how he reinterpreted the forms in the original into his own form of art.

It is stunning to think that Picasso, one of the world's foremost and best known artists, who is really the father of new, complete forms of art would create so many versions of a painting that he was reinventing. Picasso is and was one of the great artists of all time and he was into reinventing art.

This brings up another issue about the idea of reinvention. It is probably never finished because when you finally get your product to market, it is time to reinvent it if you want to stay in business.

In Picasso's case, he reinvented himself from a conventional artist to an avant-garde artist by creating new fields, like cubism. As he became more radical he not only answered the question of what if, but he also created his own market. So he also answered the question of who cares. Based upon the price of his paintings he also created a reasonable market at the time he was painting and has created a huge legacy market in the resale of his products.

Las Meninas by Picasso generated about 58 paintings or reinterpretations of the original. He changed colors, relative positions and format. Size also changed but the groupings of people remained relatively intact.

There are many views of Picasso as an artist, but studying his reinterpretations of Las Meninas will bring about a new and important understanding of the concept and implementation of reinvention.

LESSON

Successful reinvention never stops. There are many ways to reinvent yourself or your product. You can change styles or refine the product itself.

CHAPTER 27

Example of
Print on Demand

The advent of digital printing has changed the publishing industry dramatically. This is a classic case of creative disruption that has itself been disrupted. As printers rapidly evolved in terms of capabilities and quality, the industry began to change. At one point, a business would have a printer, a copier and a fax machine as well as a scanner and these were all necessary machines. Over time these functions were assembled into one machine. At the same time the capabilities began to change rapidly so that people could begin to develop alternative strategies for the printing of documents. In many cases, as the basic printing engine became easier to build, manufacturers developed higher-quality devices. Some of these devices were niche specific. An example is a photo-quality printer that uses photo paper and makes high-quality prints of photographs.

Eventually, printers became so cheap and easy to use that a wide variety of technologies and industries were disrupted.

One such industry was the book publishing industry. Tradition dictated that a book would be published after the author connected with a major publisher and the publisher (after significant painful steps) would have a book ready to be produced. The publisher would decide how many copies to print. The book would go to the printer who would use an offset press and print the requisite number of copies. These copies would then go to the binder who would put the covers around the printed matter and the books would go to the warehouse where they would then be sent out to the appropriate book stores.

This is a good way to print a book and this model is still in use today.

However, the advent of digital printing allowed the business model to change. The disruption is the ability to print high quality copies without the use of an offset press. The tradeoff is that the per page cost of digital printing is higher than the per page cost of offset printing. Thus, if you are going to make a large print run, it is better to use offset printing. However, if you are going to run limited print runs then it is better to use digital printing because you save the one time setup charges associated with offset printing and instead pay a higher per page cost.

These tradeoffs led to the establishment of businesses that cater to the production of limited run books, lulu.com and createspace.com. These businesses use digital printing and can print as few as one book at a time to fulfill the need for book printing on demand.

The advantages of print on demand include: quick turn-around, quick setup using simple editing and preparation tools, ability to avoid inventory and very little spoilage from unsold books. Due to these advantages, many publishers have gone to the strategy and only print in limited, even single copy volumes.

The technology has expanded into other areas as well. Many museums provide print on demand copies of art work or posters.

Further, the print on demand capability has expanded the ability of authors of specialty books to reach audiences they could not cost-effectively reach through mainstream publishers. This has created the growth of a new industry composed of self-published authors. The number of books in print has literally exploded in the last couple of years. Further, an entire industry has grown up to assist in such self-publishing. The effect has become so large that you can even print a single copy of a book that contains pictures documenting a family event, like a vacation, if you choose. Even traditional publishers have begun to use print on demand for books that would normally have fallen out of print due to lack of volume demand. Such books can be printed as needed.

The advent of eBooks and the Kindle further impacted the book publishing industry by further disrupting the business model. The initial push by Amazon using the Kindle has been further extended via iBook and Google books pursuing eBook strategies. But, this may not signal the death of traditional brick and mortar book stores.

This disruptive technology is available to brick and mortar stores who can find ways to order and download to user devices books from Google books. Larger book stores can also produce hard copy books on demand while you wait using the amazing Espresso Book Machine which will print your book from an electronic file.

Product and service positioning in the publishing industry is going to be very tricky due to the rapidly evolving business model. However, the real impact is that the number of books available has increased rapidly and you should expect this trend to continue into the indefinite future.

LESSON

As society/culture changes, new opportunities for profitable reinvention appear—and this is happening at the speed of the Internet. What will work at one time point will be obsolete faster than you think. Businesses must reinvent themselves or be marginalized.

CHAPTER 28

Example of
Digital Cameras

The photography business was a vibrant and successful business. The business model was pretty simple. You sold cameras and you could then sell processing and printing of the photographs. Numerous companies made large amounts of money in this business. One of the key issues from a user perspective was the issue of immediacy. You would go on a vacation, take large numbers of rolls of film, come home, get them developed and finally get to see your pictures. There were a variety of formats and print sizes available as well as options like slides that could satisfy a number of people's desires.

Polaroid introduced the instant camera. With this camera you could immediately develop the picture but the picture quality was not very good and the color would fade over time.

Companies such as Kodak, Polaroid and Nikon made fortunes in the photography business.

In early 2012, Kodak had fallen to the point it was in bankruptcy. It was a victim of technology reinvention.

Around 1975 in the labs of Kodak, a charge coupled device

(CCD) was used to collect and retain an image. This development was the beginning of the digital camera revolution. There are two primary sensors used to replace film in digital cameras: CCD and CMOS (complementary-symmetry metal–oxide–semiconductor). The advent of digital cameras, although messy at the start, is a really simple idea. Replace film with a sensor and storage device (that can store the information from the sensor) and you can replace film. The electronics in the camera are not overly complex and the advances in the electronics industry make the digital camera a high growth disruptive technology.

At first there were some quality issues, but over time the digital camera eliminated the film camera and only recently the last roll of Kodachrome film was shot and processed.

LESSON

Recognize technologies that can be reintegrated into new markets. Increased capability of mass storage and a substantial drop in cost have made it possible for digital photography to make every amateur a potential professional. Big brother is really watching you when "film" is free. You must evolve rapidly in environments when there is a massive disruptive change in the technology and its potential application.

The advantages of the digital camera are numerous. You can take as many shots as you want, view your photos instantaneously and delete the ones that you do not like. No messy developing. You can now edit your shots with the use of software like Photoshop which allows you to print or store them in a number of different ways. Technology has grown to where you can share photos with other people or print special photo or memory albums. And, you can post your images to a variety of web sites.

This disruption is easy to understand and tracing its roots and results is fairly straightforward.

Consider this simple what if question. Can an electronic mechanism retain or capture an image? If so, can we make a camera device that is economical and produces high quality pictures? And, if we can, will there be a huge market? The answers played out so rapidly that the result essentially killed the film business and enabled the widespread production of not only cameras but devices (phones and tablets) that contain the function of a camera. A further revolutionary side effect is the development of cameras that can take still images and also operate as video cameras. Additionally, most personal computers now contain video cameras.

CHAPTER 29

Example of
High School Strategy

People understand reinvention in a variety of ways. In one case I became aware of reinvention by a high school teacher. In the previous chapter I talked about how you could remake a simple nursery rhyme like Little Bo-Peep. But, this idea has more general applicability.

In a high school current events civics class, a teacher used reinvention for daily discussion. The strategy was very simple. Take the newspaper and pick any current event story. And, by using the article as your starting point, try to find comparable events from the past. See how many events you can identify. With a list of events, you can then analyze the current event in terms of past events.

The trick is to take the current event and analyze it in the context of what has happened in the past. The questions that you are trying to answer involve how the current event could play out. How do the current and past events differ and what could the differences or similarities mean for the future evolution or result of the event. This is just a variation on our three basic questions. We are using the current event to generate a list of similar past events.

Using the list we look at what happened and ask what if the current event followed the direction of any one of the past events followed. In this case we are using the past to set up our what ifs. By finding a set of past events that are similar and using their properties to set up new possible scenarios, we define possible outcomes. Then we can ask if anyone cares about any of the potential outcomes we have defined. This allows us to develop a set of possible outcomes and examine the relative possibility of there actually being an occurrence. This is difficult to figure out. Whether something is actually possible is biased by an analysts' personal experience or desires. In the case of wars, many people doing the analysis can be blinded by their desire to achieve a specific outcome. Thus, we can have a situation where blindness leads to an inability to think critically. So a little adventure could turn into a big deal in terms of cost or time.

With your set of possible outcomes you can develop cost estimates or economic benefits of the scenarios under consideration. Not all events will have a cost or economic benefit. Some events will just become a discussion point or a potential event. But, in many cases the events being conjured up have the potential to actually occur and there will be a cost associated with being the most probable outcome.

The strategy can be applied to a number of tasks. It is just a variant on trying to develop alternatives. In my experience the most probable future events will have a simple explanation or relationship to past events.

In many cases the basis of such an event is within a very few key aspects of past events and if you are able to find parallels to these few key events then you will get a good result. Multiple events that occur with similar results give you an understanding of the region that you can expect future events to occur within. For example, you can calculate the average change in the Dow Jones Industrial Average and determine its probable daily range to a specific day of the year in terms of percentage range compared to the previous day's close. Another example is people's reaction to a price change in gasoline at the local service station.

Variations on this strategy are rather common. It is said that Buddy Holly wrote his song "That'll be the day" after hearing John Wayne say that phrase in the movie, "The Searchers." The writing credits for the song go to Buddy Holly, Jerry Allison and Norman Petty. (Author's note: It is generally believed that Petty only helped produce the song and was not an author.) "That'll be the day" was a catch phrase used repeatedly by John Wayne during the movie that Holly picked up and used to start the song. The song had great commercial success and charted in both the US and the UK in 1957. Even though the song is a rock and roll classic it is probably most famous as the first song recorded by The Quarrymen in 1958. The Quarrymen later achieved fame and fortune as the rock group, The Beatles.

The strategy of picking up someone else's catch phrase or a current event is very common in music. In his biography, Keith Richards recounts how the Rolling Stones would reinvent songs from things they saw in common places or previously recorded songs. The Stones' song "As Tears Go By" is said to be based upon a title reinvention of the standard "As Time Goes By" from the movie Casablanca. The song is considered the first original composition of Mick Jagger and Keith Richards. Originally, the song title was "As Time Goes By" and the Stones' Manager Andrew Oldham changed it to, "As Tears Go By." The song was out of the Stones' normal genre. The Stones were generally considered a scruffy R and B band and this song was considered a ballad. The song was and is a very large commercial success.

The idea of using a previous idea for inspiration in art, music and drama is common. Examples include "West Side Story" inspired by Shakespeare's "Romeo and Juliet" and more explicit Hollywood examples such as movie sequels. Some movie sequels even go so far as to use similar introductory sequences, as in the James Bond series of movies.

In his biography, Richards talks about how the Stones and other groups used this reinvention technique to pump out songs to keep up with commercial demands and competition from other groups. In particular, he claims that when they needed inspiration The Beatles would sit around and open newspapers to search for inspiration from headlines.

Another issue illustrated by the Beatles and Stones is product positioning. Because the Beatles were viewed as a clean living well-mannered band, the Stones tried to create an image of a dirty, scruffy, wild and crazy party band. The idea was to establish a strong differentiation from the Beatles in terms of image so that the Stones could appeal to a completely different audience and hopefully ensure success.

LESSON

Rarely is profit generated by one size fits all. Pick a specific customer need to satisfy. Once successful, you can use reinvention to spread the solution to other niche areas. Do not be afraid to copy or extend related concepts.

CHAPTER 30

Example of iPod

The iPod and its relatives the iPhone and iPad provide a critical view of reinvention. Based upon his quote from the introduction of the iPhone, Steve Jobs clearly understood the issue of reinvention. He clearly states that Apple is reinventing the phone. There is no doubt that the iPhone was intended to be an improvement and reinvention of a conventional smart phone. However, Apple had been a reinvention company for numerous years. Even though there are Apple competitors who viewed Apple as not being very good at marketing, Apple clearly has been successful and today stands as the prime example of a company that produces quality products for the high technology customer.

At the start, Apple primarily made computers. The early products focused on providing users with basic capabilities in an easy to use format. A key issue is that their products were customizable through the use of slots. This feature went away with the Mac as it became more complex. Yet the capability of customizing your product took a turn for the better with Apple's recent products, particularly the mobile products, with the ability to add applications.

In this chapter we will look at the mobile products and their overall strategy.

We start with the iPod. Portable music devices were not a new invention. Not too far back in history, we should note that there were devices that used different forms of content. For example, the Sony Walkman and its competitors used cassette tapes. The Sony Discman and its competitors used compact discs. Thus, the idea of portable music devices was not really new. In the case of cassette tapes, you generally played tapes that you bought at a store as very few people owned the capability to copy a tape.

As personal computers became ubiquitous and music migrated to compact discs, the quality of sound improved as well as the ability to back up and share music. Still the majority of music was store bought. As people began to have the ability to copy compact discs, the ability to store music files on the computer became easy.

About this time you also had the idea of digitizing music to ensure that the file size was minimized. This led to the invention and introduction of another portable music device, the MP3 player. The first-announced MP3 player was in 1996 by Audio Highway; it announced the Listen Up player. Although as early as 1979 others had demonstrated personal digital audio players, Listen Up provided a way to interface to your computer, similar to how products work today. Apple entered the field in 2001.

A big problem for the music companies was that given MP3 files (or other file formats) you could easily share music. In fact, the advent of the peer-to-peer file sharing system from Napster was causing the music business severe financial hardship as consumers set up file sharing networks where you could go to the Internet to find and download songs for free. No longer did you need any real special equipment to access large amounts of musical content.

What Apple brought to the party was a brilliant idea, the idea that you could construct a system that would allow users to store and use their own music while providing an online capability to buy individual songs from the music content providers: iTunes.

Apple's disruption is simple: marketing. They provided (and thus were able to convince the music publishers to go along with their scheme) the ability to keep the music you already owned without paying any more money and also acquire new music that you wanted on a song-by-song basis. This is a disruption! Because of its low cost it diminishes the impetus to steal music. As the music suppliers signed, on Apple caused a complete change in the way music was stored, sold and distributed. It was iTunes as a store that let the iPod dominate the portable music player market. I admit that the iPod had a set of interesting technical features compared to the competition, but the genius was in the marketing and positioning of the content. Part of the issue was digital rights management, but as an issue that quickly went away.

Not to be too cavalier about the products that have let Apple dominate the market, but the iPhone is simply a smart phone with a clever user interface similar to the graphical user interfaces of the Mac. Further, the iPhone and Apple created the concept of having lots of applications available that the user could download via the already established iTunes mechanism. Again, it was a clever device with clever features well positioned from a marketing standpoint. And, the iPad is just a big iPhone with a choice of where you get your connectivity, including the ability to use Wi-Fi to potentially obtain free connectivity.

I do not in any sense mean to minimize the ability or difficulty of building and conceiving of the three products, but from a disruption point of view they are really reinventions of two basic system ideas: the MP3 player and the smart phone. But, the genius of Apple was in the marketing and content development relationships they created.

Getting practical devices such as these also depends a lot on the design of the user interface and practical hardware issues such as battery technology.

LESSON

Collaboration and new trends can provide massive opportunities. Sometimes everyone must compromise to achieve a mutually acceptable goal. Reinvention is not done in a vacuum.

CHAPTER 31

Discussion of the Future

Before we leave this part I wish to comment a little on the subject of mobility. Mobility is the future—mobility empowers multi-tasking, one of the upcoming fields. As we become more dependent on the Internet and digital electronics, mobility becomes an expected part of our experience and culture. There are a set of key technical issues in this area. First, weight is a critical factor in a product. Second, battery life is a key issue in a product. Third, connectivity is key in a product.

If we can make changes in these parameters, we can begin to develop products that we can free from their tethers and we can begin to modify the way we do business. One of the key issues that we must address is what types of capabilities should we put in new mobile products? We have to make decisions about their capabilities. A decision on capability dictates the level of weight and power we need. The need for connection is dependent on how general purpose you want to make the product. For example consider the Kindle versus the iPad. The original Kindle was smaller, lighter and had a bigger battery life than the iPad. But they got this capability by limiting both the function and the type of screen.

Over time both devices morphed and now they are going

head to head.

Apple tries to morph their product by making it more functional. They are planning and hoping that the apps (applications) will keep their sales rising against all competitors.

Kindle, on the other hand, has chosen a strategy of not only reinventing the Kindle but of morphing it simultaneously in different directions. This is a key strategic difference.

Apple is reinventing their basic device making the device better from a hardware point of view while increasing the availability of apps. Kindle is reinventing with new top of the line devices and models that add fancier screens and functions. But Kindle continues to position their product as an entertainment device emphasizing books, movies and games. Apple envisions a single broad capability platform.

Both devices have shown a propensity to capture the mass consumer market although Apple generates more buzz than Kindle.

Apple has also extended video conferencing and phone-like functions to the iPad as a distinguishing feature of the product.

Because of established and entrenched positions, both devices are in a good place to try and fend off competitors who try to enter the mobile market. The iPad and Kindle have essentially put a stake in the ground between the capabilities of a phone and a laptop or netbook.

It is the evolving use of this technology platform that makes it difficult for other devices by other manufacturers to break in. The Kindle has the advantage of being very easy to use. The iPad has the advantage and is positioned as a simple computer as well as an entertainment device.

Kindle fragments the market space with specific functions and price differentiation whereas Apple fragments the market space with its overall capabilities.

Will Kindle reinvent itself with higher functions? Clearly they will as their tendency is to increase functions and lower prices on less capable devices.

Will Apple come up with a new device that brings more functions into the mainstream of mobile capabilities?

At this point we do not know the answers to these questions. We do not know the direction that Apple and its competitors will take or the future direction that devices such as the Kindle will take. We do not know the future competitors. But we do know that mobility and higher functioning devices are in our future and this is a field that is ripe for reinvention from the device batteries to the device functions to the software that runs on the devices. This will be a major field for reinvention for years to come.

LESSON

Opportunity abound! More inventions and a more complex society increase your opportunity to create reinvented products.

Part IV Conclusion

We have made a brief trip through a set of examples discussing disruption and found that it is not good enough to have a wild and crazy idea if it is not practical. We also saw that even good ideas do not lead to success if they do not create a mass market. It is the combination of a reinvented idea plus a good market and great product definition coupled with good marketing that will get you into a successful position. This is where you grab the brass ring!

PART V

COMMENTS ON FUTURE DISRUPTION

For years I have had discussions and debates with people on what it means have an innovative idea, be an innovative person or what makes a product innovative. There are books written on how you can be innovative just as there are books written on how to be successful. However, innovation is a very complex thing and it is really difficult to define and quantify until after the fact. If you are an innovator in an area that has no real market potential your innovative solution will never be recognized or be commercially successful (generate revenue and create wealth).

My thinking about innovation is that it is useless unless it involves the creation of products that have the potential to be sold in the commercial marketplace. In my view innovation must result in products that can be sold. Something is innovative only if It results in a product! You want to produce concepts that are salable. You want to produce products that are sustainable. You want to evolve them to remain in business.

CHAPTER 32

Discussion of Future Reinvention

Generally, successful products are developed through product reinvention. To understand this reality is to look at products with an eye to their market potential. Do not get hung up over the issue of how much they advance the state of the art. We want to consider how products disrupt the market. Products that are highly disruptive will tend to have higher sales than products that do not disrupt the market. But, we want to focus on products that can generate profits not just sales.

I want to look for products or changes that will disrupt the status quo and then see how they can evolve over a period of time to ensure market dominance. It is not a philosophical issue for me to take an existing product and/or concept and use it as a beginning for a new concept or product. In fact, it is preferable. This way I know things about the market and how to position a set of products when I'm contemplating inventing something that is innovative or new.

There are a lot of areas that are ripe for new invention today. From the perspective of a computer person there is the whole issue of mobility and evolving forms of social networks. But beyond that there are lots of potential areas ranging from food to transportation to changes in society. Where you will find your product or service that you can develop or use to disrupt the status quo we do not know. What we do know is that the more complex society becomes, the more opportunity there is for people to develop and exploit new ideas. There is, however, a huge market for products based upon efficiency—doing more with less (less energy, less up-front investment, less pollution, etc.).

At the same time, people who are generating the ideas need to understand that the implementation of their ideas may impact negatively the lives of others. Some advances in technology will create changes that some part of the population considers unacceptable. You as an innovator or disruptor need to understand your position on where your product fits and what changes it will make. But, you also need to understand that if you can conceive of the new product someone else can also conceive of a similar product. Whether you act or not will not save society from the potential impacts (good or bad) of a new product.

I suggest that the way to develop new products and build successful companies is to embrace change and to be the person who causes disruption. You want to create positive disruption. You want to innovate and create positive quality of life improvements. You do not want to be the person who is displaced by innovation. You should seek disruption as a way to ensure your future because not seeking to create innovation and disruption will doom you to living in the past.

Part V Conclusion

Create! Reinvent! Position! Disrupt!

Simple innovations yield positive results!

Do not make buggy whips!

APPENDIX

A mapping of tinyurl URLs to full URLs is provided below:

1. Macworld Expo: Jobs Unveils the iPhone, Peter Cohen, Macworld, January 9, 2007.

    http://tinyurl.com/7wqhlp4

    http://www.pcworld.com/article/128474/macworld_expo_jobs_unveils_the_iphone.html

2. Reinventing The Same Mission, Lewis D'Vorkin, Forbes, November 2, 2011.

    http://tinyurl.com/7xyv9d7

    http://www.forbes.com/forbes/2011/1121/opinions-brief-word-reinventing-journalism-lewis-dvorkin.htmll

3. The Case for Product Reinvention, Jonathan Katz, Industry Week, January 20, 2010

    http://tinyurl.com/7e589ru

    http://www.industryweek.com/articles/the_case_for_product_reinvention_20843.aspx

4. The Mother of Reinvention, Patrick J. Sauer, April 27, 2009.

   http://tinyurl.com/odgzxp

   http://www.inc.com/articles/2009/04/reinvention.html

5. The Virtues of Reinventing the Wheel, Max McKeown, May 24, 2011.

   http://tinyurl.com/7wkrr7c

   http://www.maxmckeown.com/post/5806228900/
   the-virtues-of-reinventing-the-wheel

6. "It's in the Book", Johnny Standley.

   http://tinyurl.com/2vw3bd6

   http://www.youtube.com/watch?v=qQA6tBYAvms&feature=re
   lated

7. The Chinese Waiter, Buddy Hackett.
   http://tinyurl.com/749vj4q

   http://www.youtube.com/watch?v=LkduTnVSQoI

8. Holographic memories could make others obsolete, Peter L. Briggs, Computer World, August 26, 1970.

   http://tinyurl.com/7jnrvrz

   http://news.google.com/newspapers?nid=849&dat=19700826&i
   d=98ZOAAAAIBAJ&sjid=1UkDAAAAIBAJ&pg=6038,1724309

9. Frank Marchuk Laser Computer, New Scientist, December 2, 1971.

   http://tinyurl.com/7mafuqu

   http://books.google.com/books?id=s5hPWIkgZ_UC&p
   g=PA25&lpg=PA25&dq=Frank+Marchuk+laser+c
   omputer&source=bl&ots=aLkp9GteGB&sig=3qCE
   4WeElrgyhbQA-nZ8Te9cH0Y&hl=en&sa=X&ei=Q-
   IzT6rwCYXc0QHwsfDSAg&ved=0CCMQ6AEwAQ#v=onepage
   &q=Frank%20Marchuk%20laser%20computer&f=false

10. Laser computer "five years ahead", Don Riseborough, The Sydney Morning Herald, January 7, 1971.

    http://tinyurl.com/6t279dm

    http://news.google.com/newspapers?nid=1301&dat=19710107&i
    d=OvhjAAAAIBAJ&sjid=k-UDAAAAIBAJ&pg=1023,2153734

11. Frank Marchuk Laser Computer, New Scientist, December 14, 1972.

    http://tinyurl.com/7f76kps

    http://books.google.com/books?id=TCTpu1UVFsYC&pg=PA6
    80&lpg=PA680&dq=Frank+Marchuk+laser+computer&sourc
    e=bl&ots=GBnwcfhx4b&sig=SqHu4hqZQyiVfmxULwrlHnlu8
    FM&hl=en&sa=X&ei=Q-IzT6rwCYXc0QHwsfDSAg&ved=0C
    CAQ6AEwAA#v=onepage&q=Frank%20Marchuk%20laser%20
    computer&f=false

Index

Made in the USA
Lexington, KY
22 May 2012